Why wa
in the Pear Tree?

Why was the Partridge in the Pear Tree?

The History of Christmas Carols

Reverend Mark Lawson-Jones

First published 2011

Reprinted 2011, 2020

The History Press
97 St George's Place,
Cheltenham, Gloucestershire, GL50 3QB
www.thehistorypress.co.uk

British Library Cataloguing in Publication Data.
A catalogue record for this book is available from the British Library.

ISBN 978 0 7524 5957 8

Typesetting and origination by The History Press
Printed and bound in Great Britain by TJ Books Limited, Cornwall

Contents

Foreword

As winter approaches and the days get shorter and darker, the shops and streets begin to fill with Christmas decorations and lights, and before we have managed to think of cards and presents, we start hearing Christmas carols all around us – on the radio, in TV commercials and as we shop in the supermarket. Christmas carols have become part of our culture and carol services are still popular in our churches and cathedrals as we hear of the message of the birth of Jesus and how God chose to visit his people. Carols were first sung in Europe thousands of years ago, although they were pagan songs and people danced as they sang and celebrated the Winter Solstice feast, the shortest day of the year.

The early Christians took over the pagan feast as the feast of the birth of Jesus Christ and they began to sing Christian songs, most of which were written in Latin. In the thirteenth century, St Francis of Assisi changed all that when he introduced the Christmas crib as a focus of devotion and also the Nativity Plays to communicate the message of Christmas. The people in the plays sang songs in their own languages and the audiences joined in the choruses and so the tradition of Christmas carols was established and they were sung by families in homes and churches and passed down from generation to generation. When Oliver Cromwell and the Puritans 'banned' the celebration of Christmas, people sang carols in secret and then in Victorian times they were collected from the villages and sung more widely. New carols were written and people enjoyed singing carols in schools and churches and in the streets. They even went from door to door and often collected money for charity at the same time.

In 1918, Eric Milner-White, the Dean of Kings College Cambridge introduced the now famous service of Nine Lessons and Carols to celebrate the ending of the First World War. It is still broadcast today and is a feature of many cathedrals, colleges and parish churches. More recently, churches have introduced the Moravian Christingle service, which along with Crib Services are very popular with children and adults alike.

Carols relate the wonder of the Christmas story told by St Luke about the birth of Jesus, who millions of Christians all around the world today acknowledge as their Lord and God. The story of the king of kings being born in a lowly stable to a young mother far from home often contrasts with our own homes and the Christmas lights and trees and the over-indulgence of food and drink. It is so easy to get caught up in the commercialism and celebrations that we forget the central message of Christmas, that God loved us so much that he gave us his Son to live among us.

Christmas carols contain the central message of that wondrous event when angels sang and shepherds and Wise Men came to worship – and we are also invited to worship the Christ-child. We may sing the carols without reflecting a great deal on the words we are hearing, so I hope this book will provide fresh insights into what we sing and make us think more deeply of what God has done for us. Mark Lawson-Jones has done a remarkable job in researching some of best loved carols and illuminating them with stories of how they were written and what they mean. I hope this beautiful book will bring pleasure to many and also provide an answer to that seasonal question of what to give friends and relatives for Christmas.

Dominic Walker OGS, Bishop of Monmouth

Introduction

Christmas carols always seem to bring out the best in people. It's as if we can travel back in time to a place where life was less complicated and Christmas was full of joy and magic. The churches fill with people and in our villages, towns and cities people meet to stand together in the cold to sing songs. 'The Holly and the Ivy', 'O Come All Ye Faithful' or 'Once in Royal David's City' can fill us with hope for the future and renew our belief in humanity once again, even if it is a short-lived feeling.

Christmas has been a time of rest, celebration and sharing for many hundreds of years. However, as I wrote the chapters of this book I couldn't help thinking that we seem to accept so much about Christmas carols and songs without questioning. Intermingled with the Christian imagery there are frequent mentions of evergreen plants, historic dances and practices and even ritual dating back to times long before the first Christmas. Much of this seems to go unquestioned and uninvestigated. Why was the partridge in the pear tree? Who was Good King Wenceslas? And what are the pagan origins behind 'The Holly and the Ivy'?

I had always thought that many Christmas carols had their roots in the Middle Ages, but this turned out to be far from true. Whist researching this book I discovered how Christmas was nearly killed off in the sixteenth and seventeenth century, I discovered that the 'Golden Age of Carols' was the nineteenth century and I discovered carols that united soldiers on the Western Front during the First World War.

Last Christmas I officiated at the marriage of Jim and Alison Dennehy, in the historic setting of St Mary's Church, in the village of Magor, South Wales. The service took place one week before Christmas and snow was on the ground. As the celebration of Christmas mingled with the celebration of the promises they made to one another I wondered why more couples didn't opt for a marriage ceremony at this time of year. All the elements for a successful day were present; family, friends, food and drink. The Christmas carols really set the scene and made the day even more special as the couple started their married life together.

What, then, is the history of this excellent tradition of singing carols and songs around Christmas that can add so much to special occasions? When did it all start?

St Mary's Church, Magor, in the snow.

When did we start singing?

Some suggest that the word carol derives from the Old French, or Middle English *carole*, meaning 'to dance'. Alternatively, it could be related to the late Latin *choraula*, meaning 'a choral song'. Whichever root the word originates from, we can be fairly certain that the 'dancing' element of caroling was relatively short lived, and the term has come to be associated with singing in a loud and joyous manner, in the pub, at home, in church or door to door. However they appeared first, Christmas carols are a firm tradition still celebrated today. What is intriguing is that although many carols describe religious events relating to the birth of Jesus Christ, evergreen

plants such as the holly (*ilex aquifolium*) are frequently mentioned too. These facts are investigated in more depth later in this book and will point towards the rich history of carols and Christmas songs that have only really found a home in the church since the early nineteenth century. Before this, carols were more likely to be sung by wassailers and carolers in the squares, streets, pubs and homes of Britain.

It's wholly possible that the earliest carols date back to the thirteenth century. There has been some speculation that the words of 'Adeste Fideles' (O Come all ye Faithful) date back to that century, if the lyrics can be attributed to St Bonaventure, the Italian scholar. This is still quite a mystery however, and there is no firm evidence either way.

'The Coventry Carol' refers to the Massacre of the Innocents when Herod ordered all infant boys to be killed. It is a haunting lament of a mother for her child, and was written for a Mystery Play in the sixteenth century that told the story of the nativity. All the earliest manuscripts have been lost, leaving some question over the original words. There were also two other carols written for the play that would have been sung by the shepherds in the nativity story. All three would have been performed in an unaccompanied three-part harmony.

'I Saw Three Ships' was thought to have first been sung in the fifteenth century, mainly because the original tune was a variant of Greensleeves, which people believed was written by King Henry VIII. This is wholly incorrect. Henry didn't write Greensleeves; it is Elizabethan in origin and based on an Italian style of composition that didn't arrive in England until long after his death. The carol first appeared in print in Derbyshire in the seventeenth century and was reintroduced by the prolific carol collectors and editors William B. Sandys and Davies Gilbert in 1833, at what was the start of the golden age of Christmas carols. This demonstrates the mystery that surrounds almost every Christmas carol and song.

Just as a popular musician can secure his or her place in musical history with one good Christmas Hit, it appears that hymn-writers have secured their place in the Christmas hall of fame with their writing or rewriting of classic Christmas carols. From the early eighteenth century and Charles Wesley, to John Mason Neale, Christina Rossetti and Cecil Frances Alexander in the nineteenth century, their best remembered and most loved compositions have been the ones they wrote for Christmas.

As a parish priest, working as a team rector in a large semi-rural parish, I can see how, as Christmas approaches, the Church has the opportunity to serve the community by leading the celebrations in many ways. We arrange advent services in the run up to the Christmas season, as one might expect. But also, in an old Moravian service, oranges are decorated to tell the Christmas story and message, commonly known as Christingle.

Midnight Mass, as Christmas Eve gives way to Christmas Day, fills the church with revellers, anxious to sing the classic carols and get a good start to their Christmas celebrations. In addition to these events we mustn't forget the many carol services in the churches, pubs and streets. By the time the turkey is on the table, dozens of extra events have taken place, with the usual mountain of mince pies, washed down with a considerable amount of sherry and mulled wine. The celebrations and festivities all take place to the soundtrack of Christmas, the traditional carols and songs that are loved by so many. It wouldn't be Christmas without them.

In this book we are going to look at some of the best loved carols and the age-old traditions that gave rise to them. We are going to look at how Christmas was nearly stopped forever, and how today in the strangest of places, carols and songs are kept alive by groups of people who protect histories and traditions that would otherwise disappear.

Reverend Mark Lawson-Jones, 2011

1

Wassailing, Mari Lwyd and Singing in the Pub

Here we come a-wassailing
Among the leaves so green,
Here we come a-wand'ring
So fair to be seen.

Refrain
Love and joy come to you,
And to you your wassail, too,
And God bless you, and send you
A Happy New Year,
And God send you a Happy New Year.

We are not daily beggars
That beg from door to door,
But we are neighbours' children
Whom you have seen before.

Good master and good mistress,
As you sit beside the fire,
Pray think of us poor children
Who wander in the mire.

We have a little purse
Made of ratching leather skin;
We want some of your small change
To line it well within.

Bring us out a table
And spread it with a cloth;
Bring us out a cheese,
And of your Christmas loaf.

God bless the master of this house,
Likewise the mistress too;
And all the little children
That round the table go.

The history of Christmas songs, carols and traditions takes us on a journey of over a thousand years to the present day; almost everything we sing, say or do needs closer investigation to understand the rich tapestry of convention and practice. People of every generation have adopted, changed and made traditions to celebrate together in mid-winter. One of the most persistent and curious is the one we consider in this chapter. No book on Christmas would be complete without looking closely at the wassail and wassailing. It's so curious that it has its own song!

The word 'wassail' derives from an Anglo-Saxon phrase, *Waes Hael*, which means to 'to be healthy'. When Geoffrey of Monmouth wrote *The History of Kings* (1135), he told the famous story of wassail, dating back to the fifth century where Vortigern, King of the Britons, meets Rowena, daughter of Hengist, a Germanic mercenary who served him:

While King Vortigern was being entertained by Hengist at a royal banquet, the girl Rowena, Hengist's daughter, came out of an

Rowena and King Vortigern.

inner room carrying a golden goblet full of wine. She walked up to the King, curtsied low, and said 'Lavert King, was hail!' When he saw the girl's face, Vortigern was greatly struck by her beauty and was filled with desire for her. He asked his interpreter what it was that the girl had said and what he ought to reply to her. 'She called you Lord King,' answered the interpreter, and did you honour by drinking your health. What you should reply is 'drinc hail'.' Vortigern immediately said the words 'drinc hail' and ordered Rowena to drink. Then he took the goblet from her hand, kissed her and drank in his turn. From that day to this the tradition has endured in Britain that the one who drinks first at a banquet says 'was hail' to his partner, and he who drinks next says 'drinc hail'.

Unfortunately, history takes a cruel turn and eventually Rowena seduces King Vortigern, this results in the Night of the Long Knives when Hengist's men massacre the Britons

A woodcut of a man preparing for wassailing.

at a peace accord, bringing about the Anglo-Saxon invasion of Britain.

The term 'wassail' at this stage is no more than a declaration, a blessing or a wish that your host might enjoy good health. Its association with treachery and murder seems to slip away, and the term wassail remains in popular usage. It is mentioned once again in the eighth-century epic poem *Beowulf* as a toast, it's translated there as 'be of good health'.

Since the twelfth century, the meaning of the word seems to have changed from a simple greeting and was instead used to describe an important event in the life of any community or village.

Usually held around Christmas and the New Year, the wassail was a party where people would meet and drink considerable amounts of beer or cider, pledging each others' health. To be a wassailer was to be a merry maker, reveller and carouser.

Soon after this, it became traditional to have a Wassail Bowl with beer or cider, into which fine white bread and cakes were communally dipped. In the 1320s Peter de Lantoft repeated this story, portraying people drinking from the same cup with the words 'drinkhaille' and 'wassaille'. Although this cannot be proven, it is believed that this practice continued and became widespread.

Around Christmas and Twelfth Night people would travel door-to-door giving away cider, beer or other alcoholic drinks, sometimes requesting payment. It has been suggested that this might have been a way to share the alcohol whilst avoiding taxation. A song from 1550 records this:

> Wassail, wassail, out of the milk pail,
> Wassail, wassail as white as my nail,
> Wassail, wassail, in snow, frost and hail,
> Wassail, wassail, that much doth avail,
> Wassail, wassail, that never will fail.

This song was used to accompany the Wassail Bowl as it travelled around the village on the cold winter's nights to encourage the participants as they shared good health with their friends and neighbours. The bowl, which was by now traditionally decorated with ribbons and evergreens and sprigs of rosemary, was carried by young girls singing songs.

It appears to have been around this time that the tradition took another route. In South-West England (Devon, Somerset, Herefordshire, Gloucestershire) and South-East England (Essex, Sussex and Kent) wassailing became associated with singing and drinking the health of trees in orchards, in the hope that they might thrive and produce a bumper crop at harvest.

Wassailing apple trees with hot cider on Twelfth Night.

In the orchards, villagers would gather, usually on Twelfth Night, and select a King and Queen in elaborate ceremonies. The pair would then be led to the trees where bread soaked in cider from the bowl, would be placed by the royalty on the branches. Whilst this was being done, the other villagers banged pots and pans and sang, beating the tree with sticks also to wake it up from its winter sleep.

Apparently, the tradition was first recorded at Fordwich, Kent in 1585 and it appears in Devon in the 1630s according to a poem by Robert Herrick:

> Wassail the Trees, that they may bear
> You many a plum, and many a pear.

Later it features quite frequently in the diary of a vicar who ministered to congregations in Sussex in late seventeenth century.

The tradition was both regular and widespread, taking place each year around Christmas time in the fruit growing areas of Britain.

Another rhyme begins, 'Here's to thee, old apple tree, That blooms well, bears well. Hats full, caps full, Three bushel bags full, An' all under one tree. Hurrah! Hurrah!' There is some disagreement amongst some historians as to whether this wassail derives from pre-Christian ritual or whether it is an extension of the village wassail, from the Middle Ages. The eleventh edition of the *Encyclopedia Britannica* states that:

> What is popularly known as wassailing was the custom of trimming with ribbons and sprigs of rosemary a bowl which was carried round the streets by young girls singing carols at Christmas and the New Year. This ancient custom still survives here and there, especially in Yorkshire, where the bowl is known as 'the vessel cup,' and is made of holly and evergreens and trimmed with ribbons. The cup is borne on a stick by children who go from house to house singing Christmas carols. In Devonshire and elsewhere it was the custom to wassail the orchards on Christmas and New Year's Eve. Pitchers of ale or cider were poured over the roots of the trees to the accompaniment of a rhyming toast to their health.

The bowl itself could take many forms; many were very ornate, decorated with birds, berries, oak leaves and other figures, though earlier bowls were much plainer. The wassail song of the Gower, in South Wales, mentions that the bowl was made of an elderberry bough, and the Welsh Folk Museum in St Fagans is home to one that is made of a wood called guayacan or *lignum vitae*, translated from the Latin as 'Wood of life', known for its extraordinary strength, density and toughness. In Jesus College, Oxford, there is a wassail bowl that can hold almost ten gallons of drink.

In one wassailing song, the singers tell that their bowl is 'made of the white maple tree'. White maple is a completely tasteless wood, commonly used even today to make some kitchen utensils and it is likely most simple peasant wassail bowls were made from white maple. There are also surviving examples of puzzle wassail bowls, with many spouts. As you attempt to drink from one of the spouts, you are drenched from another spout.

In the last few centuries the wassail has changed from merely drinking the health of your hosts, and has even become more than the blessing of trees; 'The Gloucestershire Wassail' carol, celebrates the traditions of dipping toast into the bowl full of ale, but it also asks for a blessing on their animals and staff too.

Wassail! wassail! all over the town,
Our toast it is white and our ale it is brown;
Our bowl it is made of the white maple tree;
With the wassailing bowl, we'll drink to thee.

Here's to our horse, and to his right ear,
God send our master a happy new year:
A happy new year as e'er he did see,
With my wassailing bowl I drink to thee.

So here is to Cherry and to his right cheek
Pray God send our master a good piece of beef
And a good piece of beef that may we all see
With the wassailing bowl, we'll drink to thee.

Here's to our mare, and to her right eye,
God send our mistress a good Christmas pie;
A good Christmas pie as e'er I did see,
With my wassailing bowl I drink to thee.

So here is to Broad Mary and to her broad horn
May God send our master a good crop of corn

And a good crop of corn that may we all see
With the wassailing bowl, we'll drink to thee.

And here is to Fillpail and to her left ear
Pray God send our master a happy New Year
And a happy New Year as e'er he did see
With the wassailing bowl, we'll drink to thee.

Here's to our cow, and to her long tail,
God send our master us never may fail
Of a cup of good beer: I pray you draw near,
And our jolly wassail it's then you shall hear.

Come butler, come fill us a bowl of the best
Then we hope that your soul in heaven may rest
But if you do draw us a bowl of the small
Then down shall go butler, bowl and all.

Presenting the Wassail Bowl.

Be here any maids? I suppose here be some;
Sure they will not let young men stand on the cold stone!
Sing hey O, maids! come trole back the pin,
And the fairest maid in the house let us all in.

Then here's to the maid in the lily white smock
Who tripped to the door and slipped back the lock
Who tripped to the door and pulled back the pin
For to let these jolly wassailers in.

Whatever its origins, wassailing, the wassail and wassailers have quite a history in certain parts of Britain. It would also be wrong to assume that it has been confined to the south of England.

In parts of Northern England, according to the book *British Popular Customs Past and Present* (1876) villagers in Cumberland on Twelfth Night would celebrate the end of the Christmas holidays by meeting together in a large rooms and begin dancing at seven o'clock. When they stopped dancing at midnight, they would sit down to a meal of lobscouse (beef, potatoes and onions fried together); and ponsondie (another name for wassail or wael-hale or ale), warmed with sugar and nutmeg, into which roast apples are placed. All the villagers would pay an equal share for the food and drink.

Similarly, it appears that the tradition of singing at a wassail was considerably stronger in the north of England. The first recorded wassailing carol, 'Here we come a-wassailing' (found at the beginning of this chapter) was first published in the 1871 *Oxford Book of Carols*, and originated in the north of England. It is a lively piece in a 6/8 time, with close harmonies, giving the pace for the dancing.

The Mari Lwyd

In Wales, the tradition of the wassail sat comfortably with local traditions. In Kidwelly, a custom called Perllan was popular. A small rectangular board was carried around the village on New Year's Day by young men, the board had apples affixed to the four corners and a minature tree with a bird on it in the middle. They were accompanied by a large wassail cup of beer. The song included the words:

> And with us we have a perllan
> With a little wren flying in it
> He is the king of all birds.

The links with wassailing are quite clear in Perllan. However, the really popular tradition in Wales is the Mari Lwyd. The name 'Mari Lwyd' is a colloquial form of the Welsh, *Y Fari Llwyd*, or 'Grey Mare', and is one of the most ancient traditions that the people of Wales practice to mark the passing of the old year and the darkest days of midwinter.

The Mari Lwyd is a horse skull with a sprung lower jaw, mounted on a pole, which is covered in a white sheet; leather reins with bells are held by the leader, who carries a stick for knocking on doors. The revellers challenge householders to a singing contest in Welsh. In a nutshell, the Mari Lwyd is wassailing par excellence. It brings out the raw Welsh talent for singing, that to this day continues in the hundreds of male voice choirs and church and chapel choirs dotted all over Wales.

On New Year's Day (*Dydd Calan* in Welsh) householders knew that the Mari Lwyd wassailers would be calling and would plan their defence in advance. They would either ply the visitors with alcohol or food, or they would challenge them to a choral contest. A joker, who would visit all kinds of practical jokes on householders who tried to avoid the revellers, would usually accompany the Mari Lwyd party.

In its purest form (still to be seen at Llangynwyd, near Maesteg, every New Year's Day) the tradition involves the arrival of the horse and its party at the door of the house or pub, where they sing several introductory verses. Then comes a battle of wits (known as pwnco) in which the people inside the door and the Mari party outside exchange challenges and insults in rhyme. At the end of the battle, which can be as long as the creativity of the two parties holds out, the Mari party enters with another song.

Some examples of this are shown below:

First Round:

The Mari Lwyd party sing: 'Open your doors/let us come and play/it's cold here in the snow./At Christmastide.'

The House-holders reply: 'Go away you old monkeys./Your breath stinks and stop blathering./It's Christmastide.'

Second Round:

Outsiders: 'Our mare is very pretty (The Mari Lwyd)./ Let her come and play./Her hair is full of ribbons/ At Christmastide.'

House-holders (giving in): 'Instead of freezing,/We'll lead the Mari,/Inside to amuse us /Tonight is Christmastide.'

Or, alternatively

House-holders (Repelling invaders thus): 'Instead of freezing/ Take the Mari home./It's past your bedtime /Tonight is Christmastide.'

The Mari Lwyd custom was not fixed and variations throughout Wales were common. Sadly, by 1920, the custom had

The Mari Lwyd and The
Widders Border Morris.
(Courtesy of Mick Widder)

started to die out. Some suggested that it might have been because of the decline in the Welsh language at the turn of the twentieth century, there have also been suggestions that the decline could have been a product of the 1904 Welsh religious revival, that saw preachers speaking out against what they saw as Pagan practices, some suggest that the austerity practiced between the wars forced people to avoid such events.

In recent times, the Mari Lwyd has made somewhat of a comeback. One writer on the subject suggested that a full return to the days of the Mari Lwyd would be impossible, because the world is no longer ready for the sight of Welshmen demanding money or alcohol with menaces, being repelled by householders with the strength of their choral singing.

Mr Peter Symonds,
the Wassail Butler,
at the Mari Lwyd.
(Courtesy of Mick
Widder)

Llantrisant's Mari Lwyd custom was revived nearly two and
half decades ago by members of the Llantrisant Folk Club very
much in the style in which it was being performed when it
originally died out.

Barbara Bailey, a Monmouthshire resident, has recorded
information about the Mari Lwyd and recounts that the party
with the Mari would sing a song or a poem of sometimes
fifteen verses, then the Mari would ask, in Welsh, 'Oes bwyd
yma?', 'is there any food here?'. If the answer came 'oes', 'yes',
then the party would enter the house and the Mari would ask
one more question, 'Oes gafr eto?', 'are there any more goats?'.
Then everyone present would join in the song, whilst the
Mari would run wildly around the house, snapping at any girls
present, until it was time to eat.

Oes gafr eto?

Oes gafr eto?
Oes heb ei godro?
Ar y creigiau geirwon
Mae'r hen afr yn crwydro.
Gafr wen, wen, wen.
Ie fin wen, finwen, finwen.
Foel gynffon wen, foel gynffon wen,
Ystlys wen a chynffon.
Wen, wen, wen.

Gafr ddu, ddu, ddu.
Ie finddu, finddu, finddu.
Foel gynffon ddu, foel gynffon ddu,
Ystlys ddu a chynffon.
Ddu, ddu, ddu.

Gafr goch, goch, goch.
Ie fin goch, fin goch, fin goch.
Foel gynffon goch, foel gynffon goch,
Ystlys goch a chynffon.
Goch, goch, goch.

Gafr las, las, las.
Ie fin las, fin las, fin las.
Foel gynffonlas, foel gynffonlas,
Ystlys las a chynffon.
Las, las, las.

Gafr binc, binc, binc.
Ie fin binc, fin binc, fin binc.
Foel gynffonbinc, foel gynffonbinc,
Ystlys binc a chynffon.
Binc, binc, binc.

Is there another goat? (Translated)
Is there another goat?
That's not been milked?
On the craggy rocks
The old goat is wandering.
A white, white, white goat,
Yes a white lip, white lip, white lip,
A white tail, white tail
A white flank and tail,
White, white, white.

A black, black, black goat,
Yes a black lip, black lip, black lip,
A black tail, black tail.
A black flank and tail,
Black, black, black.

A red, red, red goat,
Yes a red lip, red lip, red lip,
A red tail, red tail.
A red flank and tail,
Red, red, red.

A blue, blue, blue goat,
Yes a blue lip, blue lip, blue lip,
A blue tail, blue tail.
A blue flank and tail,
Blue, blue, blue.

A pink, pink, pink goat,
Yes a pink lip, pink lip, pink lip,
A pink tail, pink tail.
A pink flank and tail,
Pink, pink, pink.

Although there are significant regional variations for this song, traditionally, the last goat is always pink. I have been unable to fathom why this might be. However, it is clear that there is a strong link between wassailing and the Mari Lwyd; they sit well together as culturally important events in the lives of their communities.

A mixture of the Mari Lwyd and wassail customs occurs in the border town of Chepstow in South Wales, every January. A band of English wassailers meet with the local Welsh border morris side, The Widders and the Chepstow Mari Lwyd group on the bridge in Chepstow. They greet each other and exchange flags in a gesture of friendship and unity and celebrate the occasion with dance and song before performing the '*pwnco*', or 'verbal jousting' at the doors of Chepstow Castle

A silhouette of some of The Widders dancing. (Courtesy of Mick Widder)

and several places in the lower part of the town, beginning at the Bridge Inn and then around the town. Tim Ryan, a member of the group said, 'It looked like they were marching to war, then all peace broke out.' Member of the Widders 'Mick Widder' said it's the 'newest old tradition in Wales'.

Singing Carols in the Pub

In the north of England, more specifically Derbyshire, Yorkshire and Nottinghamshire, the formality of wassailing has given way to something of a phenomenon: Mass singing in the public houses during the second half of November and all of December. It has been described as one of the most remarkable instances of traditional singing in the whole of Britain.

Local people write settings for popular carols, but also the more obscure songs that have been all but forgotten. The participants attend for many reasons; some are Christians, who see this as important as any observance of Christmas held in church; some see it as an event that helps to preserve the historic singing tradition and the ancient hymns that would otherwise be out of print and out of mind; and some attend because they enjoy singing together. Whatever the reason, the pubs are usually packed with people standing with a drink in hand, to deliver their unique repertoire of Christmas songs, both sacred and irreligious, that have become an essential part of Christmas for local people and visitors alike.

In a 1978 article of the magazine *Melody Maker* a reporter travelled to South Yorkshire to experience the event in one of the 'singing pubs'. The Royal Hotel, on the edge of Sheffield, is situated in Dungworth, a village where then 'mostly farmers, farmers' wives and their children live' and the few others who made the five-mile journey into Sheffield every day.

Carols in a Derbyshire pub.

Even though Dungworth is a small village, it was reported that the people couldn't remember a time when they didn't spend their Sundays during the Christmas period gathering at the Royal Hotel, settling down to a pint, and then proceeding to 'sing their heads off' with verve and gusto. The singing started on the Sunday after Remembrance Sunday and continued until the Sunday after Boxing Day.

After the article was published in 1978, the tradition had somewhat of a resurgence, attracting fans of folk music and others who wanted to witness a living folk tradition and help to keep it alive. The influx of 'folkies' wasn't wholly popular with some local people, believing that the tradition was sufficiently robust to survive on its own.

The 1978 report noted that the tradition had indeed survived in many of the 'singing pubs' in the area, where carols were sung with 'no airs and graces, roared out with vigour, and at a volume that could strike terror into the hearts of neatly-surpliced choirboys with piping pure voices. Loud and lusty

Singing king on
a barrel.

with no time for the sweet, lilting cadences of the carols sung
at most Christmas services. The singers in the bar, shoulder to
shoulder, pints in hand, mostly singing from memory.'

The landlady of the Royal Hotel in the 1970s, quoted in the
Yorkshire Post, said that they would need 'Three eighteens for a
good sing', meaning three eighteen-gallon barrels of beer (400
pints). A regular at the carols who was also questioned about
the events said, 'Proper carolers sing and drink, sing and drink,
sing and drink', and that he felt it was 'almost like church with
good feeling and fellowship. It's like religion with beer'.

More recently, in 2011, Dave Lambert, the current landlord
of the Royal Hotel, confirmed that the tradition is still alive
and well. He said, 'Some say that carols have been sung in local
pubs for the past 200 years, some say 400.' Commenting on
how unique the carols are, he said, 'Locally, there are twenty-
eight versions of "While Shepherds Watched" with a several
of them being sung exclusively in The Royal Hotel with
local musical arrangements that have stood the test of time'.

The singing still takes place for the same amount of time, the Sunday after Remembrance until the Sunday after Boxing Day. He was also able to confirm that the consumption of beer at these unique events has not diminished either.

The carol singing attracts upwards of 150 people, many standing outside. People travel from all over England and even further afield to witness this prime example of British culture at its best. Mr Lambert said, 'A group of people even travelled from Norway and stayed a fortnight to enjoy the singing, they took back ideas to start the practice there'.

One feature of the Yorkshire carols that is reminiscent of the Mari Lwyd and wassailing is called 'fuguing', a verse and a response pattern of singing, where people repeat the words at the end of the verses, and musically the bass line answers the melody. 'Mount Moriah', 'Old Foster' and 'Egypt' are three examples of this. Probably the most famous, however, is the musical setting written for 'While Shepherds Watched', which was borrowed for the folk song 'Ilkley Moor B'aht At'.

In some pubs the words are put on a flipchart at the front, in some books are produced, but in many places the people are familiar with many words, although the more idiosyncratic Victorian lyrics continue to produce wry smiles from the assembled carolers.

In response to a suggestion that the Sheffield Carols were dying out, a contributor to an internet forum on local arts maintained that was 'nonsense', stating there are still 'over fifty versions of 'While Shepherds Watched' being sung throughout the region, you just have to know where to look'.

Wassailing, Mari Lwyd or Sheffield Carols are all living and breathing examples of the power of custom and culture. Keeping alive the traditions of the past, bringing people together for important celebrations.

It could have all been so different though. The Puritans had other ideas about singing, drinking, dancing and Christmas.

2

The Puritans Tried
to Kill Christmas

During the sixteenth century Christmas was, as it is now, extremely popular, not only as a religious festival, but also as a time for families to take part in a wide range of traditional pastimes. Christmas music had spread from the Church, where it was found in the form of chants, litanies and hymns, to become popular songs performed throughout the land by minstrels, travelling players or wassailers, the Mari Lwyd, or just sung to simple accompaniment in pubs, houses and halls. The first Christmas carols secured the national love for them as the people danced and sang to celebrate Christmas.

The festivities saw homes and public buildings decorated with holly, ivy and rosemary. Church services were widely attended and gifts were exchanged at New Year. Seasonal food and drink would be prepared and stage-plays, concerts and events were organised for everyone. The social function of Christmas was two-fold; firstly, the struggles of a harsh winter could easily be forgotten with this welcome midwinter respite, and secondly; the Christmas season acted as a force for social cohesion, as people rediscovered their interdependence and shared the best of what they possessed. The villages and towns resonated with the sound of merriment with the accompany-

The Lords of Misrule.

ing stories of drunkenness and debauchery, promiscuity and other forms of excess. The success of Christmas, where the usual norms were suspended for a time of celebration, eventually became its downfall.

Towns, villages, colleges and noble houses, and even the royal court often chose a mock king to preside over their Christmas festivities. Temporarily elevated from his ordinary, humble rank to that of 'king', he was known by a variety of names, including the Lord of Misrule, the Abbot of Unreason, the Christmas Lord, and the Master of Merry Disports. These colourful titles reflect the kind of madcap revelry associated with these parties.

The duties of the Lord of Misrule varied, as did the type of entertainment offered over the Christmas period. The Lord's most fundamental duty, however, was to preside over the festivities as a mock king. One wealthy estate owner left a record of the authority he granted to the Lord of Misrule:

> I give free leave to Owen Flood, my trumpeter, gentleman, to be
> Lord of Misrule of all good orders during the twelve days. And also,

I give free leave to the said Owen Flood to command all and every person or persons whatsoever, as well as servants as others, to be at his command whensoever he shall sound his trumpet or music, and to do him good service, as though I were present myself, at their perils.

The Lords of Misrule presided over races through churches on hobby-horses during services, dancing through the streets and the consumption of huge amounts of food and drink. The Lord was allowed to order anyone to do anything, and at the end of the season, he was usually sacrificed ceremonially. This image of sacrificial kings who preside over debauchery is an echo of Saturnalia, the Roman festival that was undoubtedly practiced during the period of the Roman occupation.

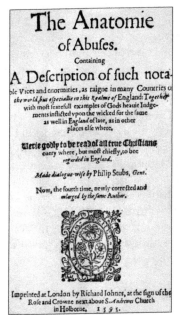

The title page of Philip Stubbes, *Anatomie of Abuses* (1580).

Around 1580, Philip Stubbes, a strict protestant expressed the Puritan view in his famed book *The Anatomie of Abuses*, when he noted:

> That more mischief is that time committed than in all the year
> besides, what masking [participating in a masquerade] and mum-
> ming [acting as a mime artist] and whereby robbery, whoredom,
> murder and what not is committed? What dicing and carding, what
> eating and drinking, what banqueting and feasting is then used,
> more than in all the year besides, to the great dishonour of God
> and impoverishing of the realm.

The whole idea of the festivities taking on a pagan tone and the misrule turning into displays of excess and deprav-ity weren't the only things bothering the Puritans, they viewed the festival as an unwanted by-product of the Roman Catholic Church.

As Christmas celebrations of this order weren't mentioned in the Bible, they believed that people weren't called by God to act in this manner. The first attack on Christmas struck on 2 September 1642, when the largely Puritan Parliament out-lawed the performance of plays, including Christmas pageants. Eventually, all stage players would be declared 'rogues' and be 'publically whipped' should they be caught.

A bill was passed entitled 'An Act for the suppression of diverse innovations in churches and chapels in and about the worship of God and for the due observation of the Lord's Day, and the better advancement of preaching God's Holy Word in all parts of the kingdom.' The bill required:

> That all alters [sic] and rails be taken away out of churches and
> chapels before April 18, 1643, and that the communion-table be
> fixed in some convenient place in the body of the church. That
> all tapers, candlesticks, basins, crucifixes, crosses, images, pictures of

saints, and superstitious inscriptions in churches or churchyards, be taken away or defaced.

Parliament enlisted the help of religious ministers to create a 'Directory of Public Worship', eventually making it the only legal form of worship. Easter, Pentecost and Saints' Days were all banned or the celebrations were drastically reduced, and the stricter observance of Sunday was called for. Puritans demanded that 'The Lord's Day' should remain only as a day of fasting and prayer.

There was a 'deep attachment to Christmas' as Historian Chris Durston commented in the magazine *History Today*, writing that:

> [The Catholic people] seem to have retained a deep attachment to Christmas during Elizabeth I's reign and the early part of the seventeenth century. The staunchly Catholic gentlewoman, Dorothy Lawson, celebrated Christmas 'in both kinds... corporally and spiritually', indulging in Christmas pies, dancing and gambling. In 1594 imprisoned Catholic priests at Wisbech kept a traditional Christmas which included a hobby horse and Morris Dancing, and throughout the late sixteenth and seventeenth centuries the Benedictine school at Douai retained the traditional festivities, complete with an elected 'Christmas King'. The Elizabethan Jesuit, John Gerard, relates in his autobiography how their vigorous celebration of Christmas and other feasts made Catholics particularly conspicuous at those times and, writing on the eve of the Civil War Richard Carpenter, a convert from Catholicism to Protestantism, observed that the recusant gentry were noted for their 'great Christmasses'. As a result, by the 1640s many English Protestants viewed Christmas festivities as the trappings of popery, anti-Christian 'rags of the Beast'.

Shortly after, on 10 September 1643, the Puritans abolished the previous liturgy and its musical accompaniment, especially

A Puritan Christmas.

in cathedrals and college chapels. At the same time, the Act abolished all archbishops, bishops, their chancellors and commissaries, and the vicar choral and chorister. Church organs were also moved from many churches.

Mr Edmund Calamy, who lived at the rectory of St Mary, Aldermanbury, preached the following on Christmas Day 1644, before the House of Lords:

> This day is commonly called The Feast of Christ's nativity, or, Christmas-day; a day that has formerly been much abused to superstition, and profaneness. It is not easy to say, whether the superstition has been greater, or the profaneness … And truly I think that the superstition and profanation of this day is so rooted into it, as that there is no way to reform it, but by dealing with it as Hezekiah did with the brazen serpent. This year God, by his Providence, has buried this Feast in a Fast, and I hope it will never rise again.

The excesses of the Tudor era had been replaced by severe intolerance and a desire to remove any celebration of Christmas. There was even a belief that giving presents to children would be damaging for them, people who continued to do so found themselves on the wrong side of the law. One minister declared that children might become 'so addicted to their toys and Christmas sports that they will not be weaned from them'.

The cultural and social consequences of the Puritan period were significant. Widespread riots and civil disobedience followed. In London a crowd of apprentices attacked a number of shops in Cheapside which had opened for trading on Christmas Day and forced their owners, 'diverse holy Londoners', to close them. In reporting the incident the weekly newspaper, *Mercurius Civicus* sympathised with the shopkeepers but argued that to avoid 'disturbance and uproars in the City' they should have waited 'till such time as a course shall be taken by lawful authority with matters of that nature'.

This 1650 note from Oliver Cromwell is found in the National Archive:

Report sent to S[i]r Hen[ry] Mildmay
The Councell haveing received severall Informations that there was avery wilfull & strict observation of the day com[m]only called Christmasse day throughout the Cittyes of London & Westm[inster] by agenerall keeping of their shops shut up and that there were Contemptuous speeches used by some in favour thereof, which the Councell conceiveing to be upon the old grounds of superstition and malignancy and tending to the avowing of the same and Contempt of the present Lawes and governm[en]t have thought fit that the Parlam[en]t be moved to take the same into Consideration for such further provisions and penaltyes for the abolishing & punishing of those old superstitions observations and meeting w[i]th such malicious contradiction of offenders in

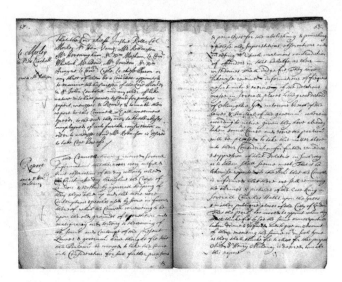

A document dating to 1650 noting Christmas 'disturbances' in London.

that behalfe as their wisedomes shall iudge fit, They have likewise
received informations of frequent resort unto and exerciseing of
the idolatrous masse in severall places to the great dishono[u]r
of Almightie God, notorious breach of the lawes and scandal of
the governm[en]t wherein according to notice given they have
already taken some Course and desire the parlam[en]t will be
pleased to take that matter alsoe into their Consideration for
further remedies & suppression of that Idolatrie in such way as
to them shall seeme meet That it be likewise reported to the
Parl[amen]t that the Councell is informed that there are still
remaining the Armes and pictures of the late King in severall
Churches Halls, upon the Gates and in other publique places of
the Citty of London That the parl[amen]t bee moved to appoint
whom they shall thinke fitt to see the same armes & pictures taken
downe and defaced and to give an Account of their executing the

The Dissenter Isaac Watts.

same w[i]thin such tyme as they shall thinke fit to allow for that purpose And S[i]r Henry Mildmay is desired to make this report.

The following year, when Christmas Day fell on the last Wednesday in the month, the day set aside for a regular monthly fast, Parliament produced the anticipated legal rulings. On 19 December an ordinance was passed directing that the fast day should be observed in the normal way. The tide had started to turn, however and even Royalist satirists and poets were writing widely published works, with titles like 'Christmas In and Out' and 'The Vindication of Christmas'.

Another similar piece, 'Women Will Have Their Will or Give Christmas His Due', which appeared in December 1648, seems to have been aimed particularly at a female audience. It contains a dialogue between 'Mistress Custom', a victualler's wife in Cripplegate and 'Mistress New-Come' an army captain's wife 'living in Reformation Alley near Destruction Street'. New-Come finds Custom decorating her house for Christmas and they fall into a discussion about the feast. Custom exclaims that:

I should rather and sooner forget my mother that bare me and the paps that gave me suck, than forget this merry time, nay if thou had'st ever seen the mirth and jollity that we have had at those times when I was young, thou wouldst bless thyself to see it.

She claims that those who want to destroy Christmas are:

A crew of Tatter-demallions amongst which the best could scarce ever attain to a calves-skin suit, or a piece of neckbeef and carrots on a Sunday, or scarce ever mounted (before these times) to any office above the degree of scavenger of Tithingman at the furthest.

When New-Come suggests she should abandon her celebrations because they have been banned by the authority of Parliament, she replies:

God deliver me from such authority; it is a Worser Authority than my husband's, for though my husband beats me now and then, yet he gives my belly full and allows me money in my purse … Cannot I keep Christmas, eat good cheer and be merry without I go and get a licence from the Parliament. Marry gap, come up here, for my part I'll be hanged by the neck first.

Mistress New-Come then informs her that if she disregards Parliament, she will be tamed by 'the honest Godly part of the army', but Custom ignores this threat, dismissing her with the rhyme:

> For as long as I do live
> And have a jovial crew
> I'll sit and rhat
> And be fat
> And give Christmas his due.

These Royalist satires were recited in market places and pubs; they were even sometimes accompanied by songs and ballads which told tales of Christmas past. Eventually, the Puritans were forced to concede that the public mood would never be fully controlled and Christmas was here to stay, 'grand festivals and lesser holy-days … are the main things which the more ignorant and common sort among them do fight for'.

The banning of Christmas was one of the biggest mistakes, one that was based on several misconceptions about the roots of the Christmas festivities, the place of carols and hymns, and the need for communal celebrations. Eventually, the people spoke. Slowly carols and hymns returned to the churches and the market places, homes and pubs, although this process was very slow indeed. The Act of Toleration restored some civil rights to Dissenters in 1689.

The Dissenter Isaac Watts' book *Hymns and Spiritual Songs* was eventually published in 1707, but the widespread celebration of Christmas with carols and songs took more than a century to properly reappear, when we started to witness the advent of the great hymn and carol writers.

At the beginning of the nineteenth century, however, something is stirring in the imaginations of poets, artists, musicians and hymn writers.

3

The Golden Age of Carols

The Golden age of Christmas carols and songs began with the rediscovery of 'The First Nowell'. It is uncertain when this carol was written. Some believe that it was written in the eighteenth century, but some music historians argue that it could have been written as early as the sixteenth century. A version of the carol was first published in 1823 in *Carols Ancient and Modern*. The book was one of many to be edited and arranged by William B. Sandys and Davies Gilbert. Sandys, a solicitor and antiquarian, and Gilbert, an engineer, author and politician, rediscovered many carols from different parts of Britain, adding them to collections, sometimes with extra verses and different settings.

Davies Gilbert was born in St Erith, Cornwall, the only child of Revd Edward Giddy and Catherine Davies. His father was the curate of St Erith Church in the village. His great love of the history and culture of Cornwall led him to assemble and write many books, including *A Parochial History of Cornwall*, he was also passionate about old Cornish carols that had all but fallen from use. He met William Sandys when he was elected to the Society of Antiquaries in 1820. In the introduction to *Carols Ancient and Modern*, Gilbert wrote:

The Editor is desirous of preserving them [the selected Christmas carols] in their actual forms, however distorted by false grammar or by obscurities, as specimens of times now passed away, and of religious feelings superseded by others of a different cast. He is anxious also to preserve them on account of the delight they afforded him in his childhood, when the festivities of Christmas Eve were anticipated by many days of preparation, and prolonged through several weeks by repetitions and remembrances.

Even though Gilbert believed he was preserving carols for nostalgic purposes, he was actually laying the foundations for one of the greatest periods of hymn, music and carol writing. By the end of the century nearly all of the carols we sing, know and love today will have been written in a renaissance for Christmas music.

CHRISTMAS CAROLS,

ANCIENT AND MODERN;

INCLUDING

THE MOST POPULAR IN THE WEST OF ENGLAND,
AND THE AIRS TO WHICH THEY ARE SUNG.

ALSO SPECIMENS OF

French Probincial Carols.

WITH AN INTRODUCTION AND NOTES.

BY

WILLIAM SANDYS, F.S.A.

LONDON:
RICHARD BECKLEY, 42, PICCADILLY.
1833.

The title page of William Sandys' book, *Christmas Carols Ancient and Modern.*

In Sandy and Gilbert's *Carols Ancient and Modern* alone we have 'The First Nowell', 'God Rest ye Merry Gentlemen' and 'I Saw Three Ships'. It also included songs and carols from far back as medieval times, many of which Sandys 'improved' and combined with other sources he found. Many of the tunes consisted of phrases that are repeated twice followed by a different phrase. These old English folk melodies were popular amongst the West Gallery Choirs, so named because at the beginning of the eighteenth century, these Georgian choirs sang in purpose-built galleries on the west ends of Anglican churches, and in Nonconformist chapels. Their fuguing tunes,

The music for 'I saw Three Ships'. (London: A.R. Mowbray & Co. Ltd, 1913)

Prince Albert, Queen Victoria and their Christmas tree at Windsor Castle. (Library of Congress, Prints and Photographs Division, LC-USZ62-117376)

unique musical meter and four-part harmonies were sometimes accompanied by the violin, cello or clarinet, although it was common for the choirs to sing unaccompanied. The Victorians frowned on this Georgian practice and sadly they removed many good examples of west galleries from churches and chapels. Nevertheless, these tunes have become popular once again, not just amongst Wassailers, Sheffield Carolers and the Mari Lwyd (see Chapter 1), but also with the choirs who have revived the tradition of West Gallery Music.

Carols were gradually making a comeback and caroling became fashionable once again, usually for raising money for a Church-sponsored endeavour. The old feast day of St Thomas (21 December) was a traditional day for caroling and became a firm favourite throughout Britain.

'I Saw Three Ships' is also thought to have been first sung in the fifteenth century, and was known across England in slightly different versions. Similar to 'The Twelve Days of Christmas' it could have been not only sung, but used as a memory game around the festive season, as people added items and attempted to remember what people had sung or said before them.

These also appear in their rediscovered form in Gilbert and Sandys' books as does the carol that is quoted in Charles Dickens' *A Christmas Carol*, 'God Rest Ye Merry Gentlemen'.

The golden age of carols also adopted hymns that were written relatively recently, and were still being sung in the churches and chapels. Charles Wesley wrote 'Hark the Herald Angels', publishing it in *Hymns and Sacred Songs* in 1739; it reappeared, re-adapted in a modified form, set to a tune by the famous composer Felix Mendelssohn and arranged by William Cummings.

'Joy to the World', written in 1719 by Isaac Watts, based on Psalm 98, received a make-over in 1839 when Lowell Mason set it to the tune we sing today, although his arrangement is very similar to music from Handel's *Messiah*.

At the same time, many other songs were being rescued from obscurity and re-arranged, including 'The Boar's Head Carol', 'The Holly and the Ivy', 'Here We Go A-Wasailling' and even 'We Wish You a Merry Christmas'.

Carols and Christmas songs had started to appear before the Victorian era, but the ascension to the throne of Queen Victoria in 1837 saw their popularity boosted. She had a strong desire to introduce a sense of seasonal morality to Christmas with the emphasis on family values at home. Christmas had, for some

time, since the Puritans, been an austere event, with carols only
being sung in a few isolated communities. However, during
Victoria's reign clergy throughout the land taught parishioners
carols and even arranged carol-singing events outside in cities,
towns and villages.

In 1840, the Queen's consort, Prince Albert, introduced the
Christmas tree to Britain. The decoration of trees at Christmas
had been an old custom in his native Germany. The custom
instantly caught the imagination of the public and heavily
decorated Christmas trees became a central part of a Victorian
Christmas.

This reimagining of Christmas took many forms, with
many of the traditions and customs we practice today beginning in this period. The tradition of giving children presents
on Christmas Eve or Christmas Day was widely popular at
this time, and despite the difficulty travelling on trains and in
carriages, relatives visited with baskets of gifts and fine food.

Carol singing in Yorkshire. Drawn by John Gilbert. (*Illustrated London News*, 1862)

The newspapers printed pictures of the Royal Family gathered around their Christmas tree, and the close-knit Victorian family would do the same, singing carols and playing games. The most popular carols of the time included 'The First Noel', 'Silent Night', and 'The Wassail Song'.

Many Victorian homes had a piano or organ in their parlours. The singing would have drifted on the air to join with the carolers and wasaillers, choirs, bells and organs in the churches. This time in history was surely the golden age of Christmas carols and songs.

4

The Coventry Carol

Refrain:
Lully, lulla, Thou little tiny Child,
By, by, lully, lullay.

O sisters too, how may we do,
For to preserve this day
This poor youngling for whom we do sing
By, by, lully, lullay.

Refrain

Herod, the king, in his raging,
Charged he hath this day
His men of might, in his own sight,
All children young to slay.

Refrain

That woe is me, poor Child for Thee!
And ever mourn and sigh,
For thy parting neither say nor sing,
By, by, lully, lullay.

'The Coventry Carol' is one that is not always familiar to those who enjoy singing upbeat and lively carols and Christmas songs. It is the lament of a mother for her son. The carol is one of the oldest still in existence and is named after the city of Coventry, where the sixteenth-century *Pageant of the Shearmen and Tailors* depicted Herod's slaughter of the innocents.

In the Bible, the Gospel According to Matthew tells the story:

> Then Herod, when he saw that he was mocked of the wise men, was exceeding wroth, and sent forth, and slew all the children that were in Bethlehem, and in all the coasts thereof, from two years old and under, according to the time which he had diligently inquired of the wise men. Then was fulfilled that which was spoken by Jeremiah the prophet, saying,
>
> In Rama was there a voice heard, lamentation, and weeping, and great mourning, Rachel weeping for her children, and would not be comforted, because they are not.
>
> Matthew 2:16-18 (King James Version)

This account of infanticide by the King of Judea, Herod the Great, reports that he ordered the killing of all young male children in Bethlehem because the Magi, or wise men, had reported that the King of the Jews had been born there. In his mission to avoid losing his throne to the Christ child, he gave the order.

The incident is described as fulfilling a prophesy made hundreds of years earlier by the Prophet Jeremiah, in the Old Testament, which is repeated in Matthew's Gospel 700 years later, 'In Rama was there a voice heard, lamentation, and weeping ...'

In the *Pageant of the Shearmen and Tailors*, the carol was a gentle lullaby sung by the women of Bethlehem to their children, before the soldiers of Herod arrived to kill them. It's a deeply sad and upsetting episode in the Christmas story, which

A relief depicting the Massacre of the Innocents.

is recounted by this carol, sung as a lament in a three-part harmony with no accompaniment.

The Pageant of the Shearmen and Tailors is one of only two plays that have survived of the late medieval Mystery Plays that took place in Coventry, the other being the *Weaver's Pageant*. The Pageant probably dates back as far as the fourteenth century and is said to be a morality play that tradesman staged for the town officials and gentry. The Pageant tells the Nativity story from the Annunciation to Mary (when the Angel tells her she is to have a son, whom she will call Jesus) to the Massacre of the Innocents.

The play's scripts would have been kept in the town hall for safekeeping, and when a copy was required, a fee would have been paid to a scribe to reproduce it, and to the town council as owners. The oldest copy of the *Pageant* that has been recorded was one that was edited by the then mayor, Master Palmer, and dates back to 1534. Unfortunately, the manuscript was destroyed in a fire in 1879. An earlier copy had been kept elsewhere, but the original text of the *Pageant* and several edited versions have been lost.

According to the English composer and pianist, Elizabeth Poston, who edited the *Penguin Book of Christmas Carols*, the 'Coventry Carol' is one of three that appear in the *Pageant*. One manuscript had a later annotation by Thomas Mawdycke, 1591, which directed that 'the women singe one' and that the shepherds sing the other two.

The only remaining evidence of the first carol is:

> As I out rode this endered night,
> Of thre ioli sheppanders
> I saw a sight
> And all a bowte there fold
> A star shone bright
> They sange teri terlow
> To mereili the sheppards
> Ther pipes can blow

The evidence of the third carol is:

> Doune from heaven, from heaven so hie,
> Of angeles ther came a great companie,
> With mirthe and ioy and great solemnitye,
> The sange terly terlow;
> So mereli the sheppards their pipes can blow.

London Evening News, Nativity Scene 1800.

In 1910, Edith Rickert, an English professor from the University of Chicago, co-authored a major book on the history of Christmas Carols. *Ancient English Christmas Carols: 1400-1700* noted the carols from the *Pageant of the Shearmen and Tailors*, joining the first and the third carols to create another which she entitled 'As I Rode Out this Enders Night':

> As I rode out this enders night,
> Of three jolly shepherds I saw a sight,
> And all about their fold a star shone bright:
> They sang terly terlow;
> So merrily the shepherds their pipes gan blow

> Down from heaven, from heaven so high,
> Of angels there came a great company,
> With mirth and joy and great solemnity,
> They sang terly terlow;
> So merrily the shepherds their pipes gan blow.

In a twist to the story, the great hymn collector William Sandys
in his book *Christmas Carols Ancient and Modern* (1833), wrote
that there is an old tradition that Herod's own son was among
the innocents slaughtered. According to Sandys, the evidence
came from his writing partner Davies Gilbert, who declared
that Prudentius, a fourth-century Roman-Christian poet,
wrote about the death of Herod's son.

There is no clear evidence that this tragedy happened; there
is evidence, however, in several sources that Herod murdered
his wife and two sons in around 7 BC, and one son in 4 BC. This
didn't stop William Sandys writing a carol about the death of
Herod's son, which he called 'When Herod in Jerusalem' the
sixth verse of which reads:

> Now mark the judgments of the Lord
> On their ungodly train,
> King Herod's son where he was nurs'd
> Amongst the rest was slain.

The tune of the 'Coventry Carol' is a Picardy third, which
is a traditional European musical characteristic used widely
throughout the Medieval period (500-1400) and even the
Renaissance period (1400-1600), and the sadness of the subject
seems to fit very well with the music in this carol with the
strangest of histories.

5

The Twelve Days of Christmas

On the first day of Christmas
my true love sent to me:
A Partridge in a Pear Tree

On the second day of Christmas
my true love sent to me:
Two Turtle Doves
and a Partridge in a Pear Tree

On the third day of Christmas
my true love sent to me:
Three French Hens
Two Turtle Doves
and a Partridge in a Pear Tree

On the fourth day of Christmas
my true love sent to me:
Four Calling Birds
Three French Hens
Two Turtle Doves
and a Partridge in a Pear Tree

On the fifth day of Christmas
my true love sent to me:
Five Golden Rings
Four Calling Birds
Three French Hens
Two Turtle Doves
and a Partridge in a Pear Tree

On the sixth day of Christmas
my true love sent to me:
Six Geese a Laying
Five Golden Rings
Four Calling Birds
Three French Hens
Two Turtle Doves
and a Partridge in a Pear Tree

On the seventh day of Christmas
my true love sent to me:
Seven Swans a Swimming
Six Geese a Laying
Five Golden Rings
Four Calling Birds
Three French Hens
Two Turtle Doves
and a Partridge in a Pear Tree

On the eighth day of Christmas
my true love sent to me:
Eight Maids a Milking
Seven Swans a Swimming
Six Geese a Laying
Five Golden Rings
Four Calling Birds

Three French Hens
Two Turtle Doves
and a Partridge in a Pear Tree

On the ninth day of Christmas
my true love sent to me:
Nine Ladies Dancing
Eight Maids a Milking
Seven Swans a Swimming
Six Geese a Laying
Five Golden Rings
Four Calling Birds
Three French Hens
Two Turtle Doves
and a Partridge in a Pear Tree

On the tenth day of Christmas
my true love sent to me:
Ten Lords a Leaping
Nine Ladies Dancing
Eight Maids a Milking
Seven Swans a Swimming
Six Geese a Laying
Five Golden Rings
Four Calling Birds
Three French Hens
Two Turtle Doves
and a Partridge in a Pear Tree

On the eleventh day of Christmas
my true love sent to me:
Eleven Pipers Piping
Ten Lords a Leaping
Nine Ladies Dancing

Eight Maids a Milking

Seven Swans a Swimming

Six Geese a Laying

Five Golden Rings

Four Calling Birds

Three French Hens

Two Turtle Doves

and a Partridge in a Pear Tree

On the twelfth day of Christmas

my true love sent to me:

Twelve Drummers Drumming

Eleven Pipers Piping

Ten Lords a Leaping

Nine Ladies Dancing

Eight Maids a Milking

Seven Swans a Swimming

Six Geese a Laying

Five Golden Rings

Four Calling Birds

Three French Hens

Two Turtle Doves

and a Partridge in a Pear Tree

One of the most complicated and curious Christmas song has to be 'The Twelve Days of Christmas'. It has attracted lots of speculation about its origins and is still the source of some dispute. Is this song a historic remnant of a parlour game, or is it a secretly coded text to teach oppressed people about faith?

In the Western Church, the twelve days of Christmas begin on Christmas Day and continue until the Eve of the Feast of the Epiphany. *The Oxford English Dictionary* defines the twelfth night as 'the evening of the fifth of January, preceding the twelfth day'. This night is traditionally the end of the

A common grey partridge.

Christmas season, the beginning of the Epiphany season, and the day when merriment would cease.

The twelve days of Christmas as a festival has a long history. It was first mentioned by one of the Fathers of the Early Eastern Orthodox Church, Ephrem the Syrian (AD 306-373), who called it a Festal Tide. At the Western Church Council of Tours in AD 567, it was confirmed as a Festival of the Church, and in the Laws of Ethelred (991-1016) it was 'ordained it to be a time of peace and concord among Christian men, when all strife must cease'.

Although the exact origins of the song are unknown, it is highly probable that it began as a memory and forfeit game for twelfth night celebrations, which would have been said and not sung. The players gathered in a circle and the leader would recite a verse and each would repeat it, the leader would add another verse, and speak faster, and so on until a mistake was made by one of the players, who would then drop out of the game. The winner would be the one who could remember all the items in order, being able to recite them at speed. The earliest printed version that suggests this was the case is found in the children's book *Mirth Without Mischief* (c. 1780).

The book contained 'Twelve Pleasing Pastimes' including 'The Twelve Days of Christmas' and the wonderfully named 'Play of the Gaping Wide Mouthed Waddling Frog sung at King Pippins Ball'. The game is certainly much older than the printed version, as the 1780 book was a compilation of games played in parts of Britain in the past.

Although there is some debate about the actual age of the game, it is fair to say that the consensus is that is dates to the early sixteenth century. This is where difficulties arise however. If the game were written 200 years before the book was printed, it wouldn't have made much sense to the British people, because partridges didn't perch in pear trees. This led some people to suggest that the game is of French origin.

The red-legged, or French, partridge perches in trees more frequently than the English common or grey partridge. The French red-legged partridge was not successfully introduced to Britain until the 1770s, long after this game had achieved some popularity. If this sounds all too far-fetched, and why shouldn't we sing about athletic British partridges sat high up in pear trees, the other piece of evidence that the original game might be French comes down to translation.

Over the years, people have noticed that the pear tree might actually be the word *perdrix*, French for partridge and pronounced 'per-dree', which was simply copied down incorrectly when the oral version of the game was transcribed. The original line would have been: 'A partridge, une perdrix.'.

The Twelfth Night.

Whichever might be correct, Madame Perdrix is almost certainly French, whether in a tree or not.

The game would have turned into a song sometime after the publication of *Mirth Without Mischief* in 1780, although Lady Gomme, (1853-1938) the prolific collector of folk tales and rhymes, described playing the game every twelfth night, before eating mince pies and the twelfth cake, a light dried fruit cake made with brandy and eggs.

Lady Gomme, in her *Dictionary of British Folk-Lore – Volume 1* (1894) points out that the festival of the twelve days, the 'great midwinter feast of Yule', was a very important one, and that 'in this game may, perhaps, be discerned the relic of certain customs and ceremonies and the penalties or forfeits incurred by those who omitted religiously to carry them out', she also adds that it was 'a very general practice for work of all kinds to be put entirely aside before Christmas and not resumed until after Twelfth Day.'

The most common musical setting for this game that turned it into a song is a popular folk tune that changes time signature throughout the song. The Roud Folk Song Index, a database of over 300,000 references to 21,600 songs, named after its founder Steve Roud, Local Studies Librarian in the London Borough of Croydon, gives the tune an index number of sixty-eight. The earliest well-known version of the music was recorded by English Scholar James O'Halliwell in 1842, which he published in his book *The Nursery Rhymes of England* in 1846. The five gold rings pivotal bars first appeared in an arrangement by the English composer Frederick Austin, which he copyrighted in 1909. In the last 150 years many different versions of this song have come to light, this isn't uncommon, as many of our favourite carols and songs are regularly set to different folk tunes.

So, we've found that the game, which turned into a Christmas song, is almost certainly French in origin, written long before the first discovered printing in 1780, and that the music is relatively recent.

The detective work doesn't end there though. There are questions about whether it is a nonsense song for children or a rhyme of Christian instruction, perhaps dating to the sixteenth century, when hidden references were placed in songs and rhymes to teach the faith to youngsters. This was a time of great uncertainty and religious strife, with the Protestant Reformation and revolt throughout Europe and the separation of the Church of England from Rome. Perhaps this rhyme or song was part of the counter-reformation that ran from the beginning of the Council of Trent (1545–1563) until the end of the Thirty Years War (1648), although Catholics were still prevented from practicing their faith openly until 1829.

'The Twelve Days of Christmas' as a catechism song would give each verse a religious significance.

Verse	Meaning
One partridge in a pear tree	Jesus
Two Turtle doves	The Old and New Testaments
Three French Hens	Three theological virtues of faith, hope and love (charity)
Four calling birds	The four Gospels; Matthew, Mark, Luke and John
Five gold rings	The 'Torah' or 'Pentateuch' the first five books of the Old Testament (The Law of Moses)
Six geese a-laying	The six days of Creation
Seven swans a-swimming	The seven gifts of the Holy Spirit; wisdom, understanding, counsel, fortitude, knowledge, piety and fear of the Lord.
Eight maids a-milking	The eight beatitudes.

A depiction of the Twelve Days of Christmas.

The Gospels according to Matthew or Luke differ slightly. Matthew's Gospel lists them as; The poor in spirit, those who mourn, those who hunger and thirst for righteousness, those who are persecuted because of seeking righteousness, the meek, the merciful, the pure in heart and the peacemakers.

Nine ladies dancing

The nine fruits of the Holy Spirit are listed in the letter of St Paul to the Galatians 'But the fruit of the Spirit is love, joy, peace, longsuffering, gentleness, goodness, faith, meekness, temperance: against such there is no law.' Galatians 5:22-3, The Bible – King James Version

Ten lords a-leaping

The Ten Commandments; You shall have no other Gods, you shall not make idols, do not take the God's name in vain, observe the Sabbath, honour your father and mother, do not kill, do not commit adultery, do not steal, do not bear false witness, do not covet your neighbours wife, do not covet your neighbours belongings.

Eleven pipers piping

The eleven faithful Apostles; Peter, Andrew, James, John, Philip, Bartholomew, Matthew, Thomas, James (son of Alphaeus), Thaddeus, Simon the Zealot (ignoring Judas of course, who was supposed to have betrayed Christ).

Twelve drummers drumming

The twelve points of the Apostles Creed; I believe in God the father, almighty, maker of heaven and earth, and in Jesus Christ his only Son our Lord, who was conceived by the Holy Ghost, born of the Virgin Mary, suffered under Pontius

Pilate, was crucified, dead
and buried, he descended
into hell. The third day he
rose again from the dead and
ascended into heaven, and
sitteth at the right hand of
the God the Father Almighty,
from thence He shall come
to judge both the quick and
the dead. I believe in the Holy
Ghost; the Holy Catholick
(sic) church; the Communion
of Saints; the Forgiveness of
sins; the Resurrection of the
body, and the Life Everlasting.'
Book of Common Prayer

Many have questioned the historical accuracy of this religious origin of the song. Some have suggested it is merely an 'urban myth', although there is little 'hard' evidence available either way. Some Church historians affirm this account as accurate, whilst others point out discrepancies that could mean the song is merely a good catchy folk tune to words that provided entertainment on the long dark January nights many years ago.

We may never know for certain, but for those who have good memories and the ability to sing a folk song in a different metre and at some speed, this is a favourite.

6

The Holly and the Ivy

The holly and the ivy,
When they are both full grown
Of all the trees that are in the wood
The holly bears the crown.

The holly bears a blossom
As white as lily flower
And Mary bore sweet Jesus Christ
To be our sweet Saviour.

The holly bears a berry
As red as any blood,
And Mary bore sweet Jesus Christ
To do poor sinners good.

The holly bears a prickle
As sharp as any thorn,
And Mary bore sweet Jesus Christ
On Christmas Day in the morn.

The holly bears a bark
As bitter as any gall,
And Mary bore sweet Jesus Christ
For to redeem us all.

The holly and the ivy,
When they are both full grown
Of all the trees that are in the wood
The holly bears the crown.

Carols and hymns never stand alone as mere songs; they all have rich origins that tell a story down the centuries. Intermingled with the Christian imagery in many Christmas carols there is also mention made of evergreen plants and historical details that deserve investigation. To properly understand these symbols and their significance, we need to dig a

Holly.

little deeper, beyond what is commonly accepted about our hymns and carols.

The carol 'The Holly and the Ivy' is no exception. In this particular carol, which is undoubtedly religious in content, the holly's features symbolize Jesus and his suffering. The holly produces a white blossom representing his purity. Its scarlet clusters of berries reflect his blood. The holly also has a sharp prickle; this almost certainly symbolizes the crown of thorns worn by Jesus at the time of his death. The question remains however, why is this symbolism used at all? It doesn't belong to Biblical text or early Christian tradition.

In distant history, we know that the Romans would send boughs of holly and ivy to their friends to celebrate the winter festival of Saturnalia, to honour the God Saturnus, the God of agriculture.

Even though the Romans left Britain in AD 410, the tradition must have been retained or adopted as a Christmas celebration because in AD 596, when St Austin and his disciples baptized 10,000 Anglo-Saxons on Christmas Day, we are told that churches and houses were bedecked for two weeks with holly and ivy to celebrate the occasion. This may well have secured the link between holly and ivy and the mid-winter celebrations.

There is also a link to pagan historical practice, where in the winter when nothing flowers, evergreen plants such as holly, ivy, fir and pine were considered to be a sign of new life, holding magical qualities to ward off evil, ghosts and lightning.

A Harleian manuscript dating back to AD 1451 includes a story of a contest between holly and ivy for the best place in the house. 'Nay, Ivy, Nay' tells us that the holly was finally victorious because the black berries of the ivy were no match for the beauty of the red berries on the holly wreath. This probably reflects the ongoing pagan relationship with holly and ivy as signs of good luck and the anticipation of new life in spring, even in the depths of winter.

St Austin.

It is suggested in *The Oxford Book of Carols* by Dearmer, Vaughan Williams and Shaw (1928) that the holly and the ivy represents the battle of the sexes, with holly having masculine qualities, and ivy feminine. The imagery could have been part of a tribal tale that developed into a dance for young men and women.

One old legend also states that holly sprang up under the footsteps of Jesus when he walked the earth to the cross and says that merely holding it brought good luck. Therefore, in old church calendars it also documented that the churches on Christmas Eve were decked (*temple exornate*) with holly.

In 1630, with the Stuarts overthrown, the Puritans banned many things associated with Christmas, not just carols, but also holly and ivy as seasonal decoration. With the Restoration, however, these things returned with added vigour. During this period, Edward Fisher refuted the Puritanical war on Christmas by publishing a point-by-point guide to celebrating Christmas in his book The *Feast of Feasts* (1649). In it he says that the season of Christmas is designed:

> ... to eat mince pies, plum-pottage or brawn in December, to trim churches or private houses with holly and ivy about Christmas, to stick roasting pieces of beef with rosemary or to stick a sprig of rosemary in a collar of brawn, to play cards or bowls, to hawk or hunt, to give money to the servants or apprentices box, or to send a couple of capons or any other presents to a friend in the twelve days.

These, and other texts, undoubtedly helped to secure the place of holly and ivy in the celebration of Christmas. A Victorian merchant in 1851 claimed that he sold 250,000 bushels of holly during the Christmas season, that's how popular it was!

So where did the carol 'The Holly and the Ivy' come from? 'The Sans Day Carol' (Saint Day's Carol), one of the many Cornish carols written in the nineteenth century, also provides a link. St Day was a Breton saint, and the 'Sans Day Carol' was transcribed from the singing of Thomas Beard, a villager in St Day, in the parish of Gwennap, Cornwall. The fourth verse is a translation from the Cornish version 'Ma gron war'n gelln':

Now the Holly bears a berry as white as the milk
And Mary bore Jesus, who was wrapped up in silk.

Chorus
And Mary bore Jesus Christ our Saviour to be
And the first tree in the greenwood, it was the holly.
Holly, holly,
And the first tree in the greenwood it was the holly.

Now the Holly bears a berry as green as the grass
And Mary bore Jesus, who died on the cross.

38   THE HOLLY AND THE IVY
(NATIVITY: LENT: AUTUMN)

1 The hol-ly and the i-vy, When they are both full grown, Of all the trees that are in the wood, The hol-ly bears the crown:

'The Holly and the Ivy'. (*Oxford Book of Carols*, 1954)

> Now the Holly bears a berry as black as the coal
> And Mary bore Jesus, who died for us all.
>
> Now the Holly bears a berry as blood is it red
> Then trust we our Saviour who rose from the dead.

This link clearly shows the ongoing importance of the imagery of holly and ivy in the Christmas season.

So, what about the carol? 'The Holly and the Ivy' itself probably dates back to the seventeenth century and was revamped around 150 years later by the famous folk music expert Cecil J. Sharp to be included in his collection of songs, hymns and carols of 1911. A choral arrangement was written by Sir Henry Walford Davies, which remains one of the most common musical arrangements we hear at Christmas. The original tune however was described as an 'Old French tune'. In the book *Early English Lyrics* by Chambers and Sidgwick (1926), there is mention of a broadside printed in Birmingham in 1710 with a version of the carol, which begins:

> The holly and the ivy
> Now are both well grown
> Of all the trees that are in the wood
> The holly bears the crown

The book *The Oxford Book of Carols* (1928) says of the carol, 'Words and melody taken from Mrs. Clayton at Chipping Camden, Glos. (Supplemented by words from Mrs Wyatt, East Harptree, Somerset)'.

In the twenty-first century it is pleasing to see that people still hold on to the tradition of placing holly and ivy in their homes. Whether it is done to celebrate the birth of Jesus Christ, the baptism of thousands by St Austin, to resurrect the midwinter festival of Saturnalia, to ward off evil spirits or to think of the battle of the sexes, it is certainly a most rich and complex tradition that still continues to this day. And the carol, 'The Holly and the Ivy', still echoes through the land, indeed throughout the world.

7

Hark! the Herald Angels Sing

Hark! the herald angels sing
'Glory to the newborn King!'
Peace on earth and mercy mild
God and sinners reconciled
Joyful, all ye nations rise
Join the triumph of the skies
With the angelic host proclaim:
'Christ is born in Bethlehem'
Hark! the herald angels sing
'Glory to the newborn King!'

Christ by highest heav'n adored
Christ the everlasting Lord!
Late in time behold Him come
Offspring of a Virgin's womb
Veiled in flesh the Godhead see
Hail the incarnate Deity
Pleased as man with man to dwell
Jesus, our Emmanuel
Hark! the herald angels sing
'Glory to the newborn King!'

Hail the heav'n-born Prince of Peace!
Hail the Son of Righteousness!
Light and life to all He brings
Ris'n with healing in His wings
Mild He lays His glory by
Born that man no more may die
Born to raise the sons of earth
Born to give them second birth
Hark! the herald angels sing
'Glory to the newborn King!'

Charles Wesley was probably the most prolific hymn writer Britain has ever produced and this hymn is one of his most famous compositions.

Wesley was born on the 17 December 1707, in Epworth, Lincolnshire, the eighteenth and last child born to Samuel and Susanna Wesley. He was educated in Westminster College, leaving with a scholarship to study in Christ College, Oxford. Whilst there he and his brother John formed the 'Oxford Holy Club' for the purposes of Christian worship, but also to organise visits to the sick and imprisoned. Soon, the group became known as 'Methodists'.

Wesley eventually became a college tutor; however, he left to be ordained as a deacon in the Church of England in 1735. Following a disastrous move to the new colony of Georgia, where he intended to work as a missionary, but became the secretary to the governor, he returned to London emotionally exhausted.

In 1738, Charles suffered serious illness and whilst recuperating met members of the Moravian Church in London. The Moravians, closely linked to the protestant Lutherans, had begun in 1730 after a time of division and uncertainty and were hoping to put down the foundations of a new church. Their evangelical zeal and concern for others inspired Wesley to re-evaluate his own life. The day after their first meeting, Whitsunday, 21 May 1738, he wrote his first hymn, 'Where Shall My Wondering Spirit Begin'. This was to be the first of over 6,000 hymns he penned.

Later that year, Christmas Day 1738, Charles Wesley preached at St Mary's Church in Islington, he also adminis-tered the chalice at Holy Communion. The next day his close friend George Whitefield said, 'We had the sacrament this and the following four days, the whole week was a festival indeed; a joyful season, holy unto the Lord'.

Stories tend to suggest that Wesley heard the sound of the bells ringing on his way to church on Christmas Day, filling him with deep happiness and enthusiasm to pen the hymn 'Hark! The Herald Angels Sing'. There is no evidence that this is the case, however it may well be true. The real question is whether this Christmas Day in 1738 was the first to be celebrated with the singing of 'Hark! The Herald Angels Sing' in its original form? It is certainly possible, as a few months later the hymn was pub-lished in the book *Hymns and Sacred Songs*, which Charles Wesley wrote with his brother John. In the following years his old friend George Whitefield shaped it into its present lyrical form.

In 1753, Whitefield altered the first line of the hymn from 'Hark how all the welkin rings' to 'Hark! The Herald Angels Sing', which although an improvement, must have irritated Wesley, who believed that heaven (the meaning of 'welkin') rang with joy, maybe like the bells he reportedly heard on Christmas Day.

Another difficulty for Wesley would have been that as a keen biblical scholar he would have understood that the 'Angel' and the 'Multitude of the Heavenly Host' in the Bible were not singing at all, they were '*Saying*, Glory to God in the highest' (Luke 2:13-14).

Quite how much this would have been a problem to Wesley we can only guess, although if he were to have seen the future

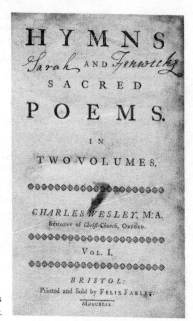

HYMNS

Sarah AND *Fenwick*

SACRED

POEMS.

IN

TWO VOLUMES.

CHARLES WESLEY, M. A.

STUDENT of *Chriſt-Church*, OXFORD.

VOL. I.

BRISTOL:

Printed and Sold by FELIX FARLEY.

MDCCXLIX.

The title page of Wesley's
Hymns and Sacred Poems.

and the countless thousands of Christmas cards that show sing-ing cherubic angels he might have complained. Both John and Charles Wesley felt strongly that the people should be edu-cated in theological issues to properly understand their faith. Charles used the words of the hymns to explain theology to people who might well be unable to read or write.

Early eighteenth-century Britain was free from the rebel-lious atmosphere that prevailed in the seventeenth century and the Industrial Revolution was yet to start. The country was becoming wealthier through trade and Robert Walpole, the first Prime Minister, had chosen a 'cabinet' for the first time. He discouraged the Church from being active, so that it would not prove troublesome to the Government.

The Church had entered a period of inaction and neglect. Daily services were discontinued in many places and the poor weren't cared for. Even though the Church remained popular amongst the people, the clergy were considered lazy and were held in contempt. Promotion was dependent on political affiliation and the church was ignored by the state that considered the churches only role to be to support the Government.

The story of this hymn is the soundtrack to the mission of John and Charles Wesley to reinvigorate the Church. Just as John's preaching would awaken much religious feeling, especially among the lower classes, the words of Charles' hymns would encourage people. As 'Methodism' spread, Charles wished to remain within the broad structures of the Anglican Church; he had never intended his work to be separate.

Even though Wesley had been reinvigorated with evangelical fervour, he was known as a sombre man, who would request slow and reflective musical compositions for his work. 'Hark the Herald' would have been sung to a completely different tune than the one we know and love today, probably the tune to 'Christ the Lord is Risen Today', another hymn written by him.

The most familiar tune for this hymn since the mid-nineteenth century is called Festgesang, composed by Felix Mendelssohn in 1840 as a cantata to commemorate the 300th anniversary of Gutenberg's invention of the printing press. Sixty-seven years after the death of Charles Wesley in 1855 the English musician William Cummings made changes so that it would fit the words of the hymn. Mendelssohn would have been as shocked as Wesley at the use of his music, the composer once said the music would 'never work with sacred tunes'.

Some carols and songs enjoy popularity for a time and then disappear from common use, however it's fair to say that 'Hark the Herald' has always enjoyed significant popularity and is sung widely still. In his *Anglican Hymnody*, published in 1885,

Mendelshohn's setting to 'Hark! the Herald Angels Sing'.

the Revd James King examined fifty-two hymnbooks in use throughout the worldwide Anglican Communion and found 'The Great Four' hymns that appeared at least fifty-one times. They were:

1. All Praise to thee, my God this night (Thomas Ken)
2. Hark the Herald Angels Sing (Charles Wesley)
3. Lo, He comes with clouds descending (Charles Wesley)
4. Rock of Ages cleft for me (Augustus Montague Toplady)

In 2006, a survey for a radio station found that the carol is still popular, ranking third in a poll of 37,000 people. Their 2001 survey put the carol at sixth place. (Classic FM 2006)

In churches, the hymn is sung at the end of Christmas services and continues to be loved by many.

8

O Come All Ye Faithful

O come, all ye faithful,
Joyful and triumphant,
O come ye, O come ye to Bethlehem;
Come and behold him,
Born the King of angels;

Refrain
O come, let us adore him,
O come, let us adore him,
O Come, let us adore him, Christ the Lord.

God of God,
Light of Light,
Lo! He abhors not the Virgin's womb:
Very God,
Begotten, not created.

Sing, choirs of angels,
Sing in exultation,
Sing, all ye citizens of heaven above;
Glory to God
In the highest.

Yea, Lord, we greet thee,
Born this happy morning;
Jesus, to thee be glory given;
Word of the Father,
Now in flesh appearing; Refrain

Many Christmas carols and songs were written in times of great struggles, political, economic or military. They often tell more than the incidents surrounding the birth of Jesus Christ 2,000 years ago, giving us a picture of the concerns of people who lived hundreds of years ago. Some carols are written in the hope that they will encourage people to solve the problems of the present, they are also a rallying call to the likeminded to stand up and be counted.

There is no better example of this than the carol, 'Adeste Fideles' that we know more commonly as 'O Come all ye Faithful'. The history of this particular carol was shrouded in

St Bonaventure.

mystery and both the lyrics and the music have been the subject of intense speculation and research for many years.

The lyrics, from time to time, have been attributed to St
Bonaventure, the thirteenth-century Italian scholar. They have
also been attributed to Cistercian monks; some have said they
are Portuguese in origin, some German and some Spanish.

The music has received no less speculation, being attributed first to the seventeenth-century English organist John
Reading, and then his son. The famous composer of operas,
oratorios and concertos, George Frideric Handel, has also
received some attention from those anxious to discover the
truth behind the music, as have many others. For a time, the
Portuguese musician Marcos Antonio da Fonseca was in the
frame, until it was realised that he was born twenty years after
the first publication of the music.

The mystery of the music and the lyrics was almost solved
in 1946, when the Revd Maurice Frost of Oxford, discovered
a new manuscript of the hymn. Sadly the cover was missing
so there were no signatures or publishing marks. The manuscript was described as a 'Choir book, Medieval manuscript
on paper. 92 leaves, written in red and black musical notation',
with a reference to '*Regem nostrum Jacobum*' ('Our King James').
Someone had also written the words '*regem angelorum*' which is
quite close to '*regem Angliorem,*' ('King of England'). The new
discovery shed a whole new light on the lyrics and music,
however with the missing front cover more detective work was
needed.

At the beginning of 1947, a Benedictine monk in Buckfast
Abbey, Devon, published a thirty-two page report, which has
almost certainly settled the matter. Dom John Stephan OSB,
started his study after the discovery of the manuscript, and even
though there were many questions left unanswered, he started
to obtain photographs of all the early versions of the carol. He
was curious about the fact that in the manuscript the mention

of King James came immediately before 'Adeste Fideles'. His attention first focussed on the discovery by the Revd Frost.

The dealers who sold the manuscript had dated it to around 1687, which if correct, would mean that the copy of the carol was at least fifty years older than any other in existence. They had decided the age based on the presence of the Jacobite statement about the King, therefore they believed it was when James II was still on the throne of England.

Dom Stephan's first reaction to this claim was that the James referred to need not necessarily be James II, but might well be 'James III', the Old Pretender, who lived until 1765, and had devoted followers all through that period. After closely examining the watermarks of the paper used for the writing, he confirmed the accuracy of his suspicion. The end-paper used for the cover bore the date '1795', but the rest of the book had different watermarks, which were traced by an expert to a period between 1720 and 1750.

The cover of Dom John Stephen's study of 'Adeste Fideles'.

The earliest copies of the 'Adeste' all bear the signature of John Francis Wade, so the next step was to examine the photographs. On looking at the first of these photographs, Dom Stephan was immediately struck by the similarity of the handwriting with that of the new 'Jacobite' manuscript. Other copies corroborated the exciting new finding.

With this new evidence, he contacted the Revd Frost to point out the coincidence. There was no escaping the conclusion to be drawn from this comparison of handwritings: the new manuscript was the product of the same scribe. Further investigation finally uncovered the scribe as a professional music-copyist who lived and worked at Douai, a flourishing town in France, twenty miles south of Lille.

In the Middle Ages, the strongly fortified town of Douai had flourished, numbering 30,000 inhabitants. Soon after, it became famous for its university, which dates from 1559, and a college founded by Cardinal Allen in the reign of Queen Elizabeth I. To English Catholics, the name Douai was recognized as the place where the majority of clergy were educated when their faith was outlawed in England. It was the place that they felt was preserving the faith, and protecting their traditions. Several other British establishments were founded there, colleges for the Scots and the Irish, and Benedictine and Franciscan monasteries. Douai was the chief centre for those who were exiled for their faith and a considerable number of English Catholics were influential in the university. Several chief posts were held by Englishmen and the first chancellor was Dr Richard Smith, formerly of Merton College, Oxford.

The scribe of the manuscript had been found, the story had taken a new turn and the story of this Christmas favourite had become intermingled with persecution, injustice and intrigue from the Middle Ages.

The scribe invariably signed and dated every one of his books with the original author of 'Adeste Fideles', the carol we know as 'O Come all ye Faithful'. With the copy discovered by the Revd Frost bearing the same text and the watermark of the paper confirming the date, Dom Stephan was confident to declare that the original author of the carol was a Catholic layman, John Francis Wade, who was born in 1711.

Wade originally wrote the carol in Latin, giving it the title 'Adeste Fideles', the following verses correspond to the English verses:

> *Adeste fideles laeti triumphantes,*
> *Venite, venite in Bethlehem.*
> *Natum videte*
> *Regem angelorum.*

> *Venite adoremus (ter) Dominum.*
> *Deum de Deo, lumen de lumine,*
> *Gestant puellae viscera.*
> *Deum verum, genitum non factum.*

> *Venite adoremus (ter) Dominum.*
> *Cantet nunc 'Io', chorus angelorum;*
> *Cantet nunc aula caelestium,*
> *Gloria! Gloria in excelsis*
> *Deo! Venite adoremus (ter) Dominum.*

> *Ergo qui natus die hodierna.*
> *Jesu, tibi sit gloria,*
> *Patris aeterni*
> *Verbum caro factum.*
> *Venite adoremus (ter) Dominum.*

Wade fled to France during the final Jacobite rising of 1745. Britain and Ireland had been in political turmoil for nearly a century, and the rising of 1745, known as 'The Forty-Five', was an attempt by Charles Edward Stuart to regain the throne for the exiles House of Stuart. Charles, known as 'Bonnie Prince Charlie' sailed to Scotland and raised the Jacobite flag at Glenfinnan in the Highlands. The army marched south and won several battles, as they gathered momentum they entered England, reaching Derby, but the battles grew harder and they were recalled to Inverness, where the last battle on British soil took place at Culloden. As Bonnie Prince Charlie fled with a price on his head to permanent exile in France, so did John Francis Wade, and many other Catholics, who believed that all was lost.

The words of 'Adeste Fideles' are a heartfelt plea for France to invade and restore the Catholic traditions and end the persecutions, led by Bonnie Prince Charlie and the secret followers of the Old Pretender James Francis Stuart, Prince of Wales, the deposed son of James II. In the words, the 'faithful' are the 'Jacobites' who are being encouraged to return, and Bethlehem, was a code for them to mean England. So this was a carol of rallying the people to return.

In his study, Dom Stephan noted that he had uncovered twenty-seven different versions of 'Adeste Fideles', and he felt that his list was 'far from complete'. He remarked also that 'One or other [version] will be found in every hymn book in the English language, and the same remark applies to hymn books in other tongues. It is probably one of the very few hymns that has found a place in every collection of Christian hymns. What greater praise could one bestow on it? And there is no sign that its vogue is likely to die out.' He goes on to write 'Another tribute which singles it out from all other hymns is the fact that, as far as the present writer is aware, no alternative melody has been attempted to supplant the original one. For these two reasons, John Francis Wade must be considered as one of the greatest hymn-writers in the world, even if he only has one composition to his credit.'

'Adeste Fideles'.

Dom Stephan concludes his study with what he calls a rather appealing version of the first verse, echoing the cries of the Jacobites.

> O hie, ye believers ! raise the song of triumph
> O speed ye, o speed ye! to Bethlehem hie!
> Born there, behold the Infant King of Angels
> O come and let us worship
> O come and let us worship
> O come and let us worship the Lord our God!
>
> (Revd Francis Trappes Richardson, 1868)

The story of the Jacobites and Wade, Bonnie Prince Charlie and Dom Stephan would be enough to close this chapter on 'Adeste Fideles'. However, the remarkable history of this particular carol doesn't end here.

Nearly 200 years after the birth of John Francis Wade, the world was plunged into war when Archduke Franz Ferdinand was assassinated on the 28 June 1914. Germany would need to meet her enemies on two fronts. When the conflict started, the German military commanders knew that the Russian Army required at least six weeks to mobilise their forces, so they concentrated on their enemies in the west by launching a strong offensive in France. Initially the French, Belgian and British forces couldn't stop them, but eventually in France they forced a stalemate and dug in for a long winter. Trenches were dug a few hundred feet apart. Soldiers spent most of their day dealing with mud and cold, guns jammed and illness was rife. If this wasn't bad enough, the trenches were little protection from sniper fire, and the machine guns on the battlefields were making this conflict one of the bloodiest in history.

One account, from Lieutenant Sir Edward Hulse read:

> It had been pouring, and mud lay deep in the trenches; they were caked from head to foot, and I have never seen anything like their rifles! Not one would work, and they were just lying about the trenches getting stiff and cold. One fellow had got both feet jammed in the clay, and when told to get up by an officer, had to get on all fours; he then got his hands stuck in too, and was caught like a fly on a flypaper; all he could do was look round and say to his pals, 'For Gawd's sake, shoot me!' I laughed till I cried. But they will shake down, directly they learn that the harder one works in the trenches, the drier and more comfortable one can keep both them and oneself.

On 17 December 1914, the first Christmas of the war, Pope Benedict XV called for a temporary truce and ceasefire on the battlefields. Germany agreed, but the other powers refused. The war had been raging for barely five months.

The trenches of the First World War.

Families had sent packages filled with cigarettes, warm clothing, gifts and medicines to the soldiers. Some of the German soldiers had also received Christmas decorations from loved ones. On Christmas Eve 1914, the German soldiers put candles in Christmas trees and decorated the edges of the trenches. Eventually, hundreds of Christmas trees appeared all across the front line. British soldiers were told to watch closely, but not to open fire.

> Time and again during the course of that day, the Eve of Christmas, there were wafted towards us from the trenches opposite the sounds of singing and merry-making, and occasionally the guttural tones of a German were to be heard shouting out lustily, 'A happy Christmas to you Englishmen!

In other areas, the two sides exchanged Christmas carols. A British soldier, Private Oswald Tilley, commented in a letter to his parents:

The *Daily Mirror* reports the Christmas Truce.

They finished their carol and we thought that we ought to retaliate in
some way, so we sang 'The first Noël', and when we finished that they
all began clapping; and then they struck up another favourite of theirs,
'O Tannenbaum'. And so it went on. First the Germans would sing
one of their carols and then we would sing one of ours, until when
we started up 'O Come All Ye Faithful' the Germans immediately
joined in singing the same hymn to the Latin words 'Adeste Fideles'.
And I thought, well, this was really a most extraordinary thing – two
nations both singing the same carol in the middle of a war.

Tilley continues his letter, 'This experience has been the
most practical demonstration I have seen of Peace on earth
and goodwill towards men'. Tilley even empathised with the
German soldiers, 'We hated their guts when they killed any of
our friends; then we really did dislike them intensely ... And
we thought, well, poor so and so's, they're in the same kind of
muck as we are.' He concludes his letter 'It doesn't seem right
to be killing each other at Christmas time'.

The singing from the trenches eventually turned into something completely different, as soldiers disobeyed their superior officers and fraternized with the 'enemy' along two-thirds of the Western Front, the 450-mile line of trenches, machine gun nests and barbed wire between the sandy dunes of the borders of Belgium and the Swiss border.

Thousands of troops streamed across a no-man's land strewn with rotting corpses. They continued singing carols, exchanged photographs of loved ones back home, shared rations, played football, they even roasted some pigs. Soldiers embraced men they had been trying to kill and agreed to warn each other if their superior officers forced them to fire their weapons, and to aim high. In his book *The Christmas Truce* (Brown) a Corporal John Ferguson is quoted:

> We shook hands, wished each other a Merry Xmas, and were soon conversing as if we had known each other for years. We were in

Deliveries of presents in the trenches.

front of their wire entanglements and surrounded by Germans – Fritz and I in the centre talking, and Fritz occasionally translating to his friends what I was saying. We stood inside the circle like street-corner orators. Soon most of our company ('A' Company), hearing that I and some others had gone out, followed us … What a sight - little groups of Germans and British extending almost the length of our front! Out of the darkness we could hear laughter and see lighted matches, a German lighting a Scotchman's cigarette and vice versa, exchanging cigarettes and souvenirs. Where they couldn't talk the language they were making themselves understood by signs, and everyone seemed to be getting on nicely. Here we were laughing and chatting to men whom only a few hours before we were trying to kill!

When news of this reached the high command it was decided that action needed to be taken. Popular urban legend would

First World War Truce, 19 January 1915.

The Illustrated London News'
coverage of Christmas in the
trenches 1914.

'The Light of Peace in the trenches on Christmas Eve: A German soldier opens the spontaneous truce
by approaching the British lines with a small Christmas tree.' (original caption)

have it that the soldiers stopped fighting to play football,
returning to battle the next day. This was not the case; soldiers
declared their solidarity and refused to fight. On both sides,
generals declared the spontaneous peacemaking as 'treason-
ous' and 'subject to court martial'. It did however take until
March 1915 to fully suppress the fraternization. By the time
of the Armistice in 1918, fifteen million people would have
been killed.

Perhaps for Private Tilley and the countless other soldiers
on both sides, the singing of 'Adeste Fideles', memories of past
Christmasses and the sense of the waste and futility of war led
in part to this ceasefire.

Each time we hear 'Adeste Fideles' we can appreciate an
extraordinary history of risings, war and death, but also those
brave people who seek an end to war and persecutions.

9

Angels from the Realms of Glory

Angels from the realms of glory,
Wing your flight o'er all the earth;
Ye who sang creation's story
Now proclaim Messiah's birth.

Refrain
Come and worship, come and worship,
Worship Christ, the newborn King.

Shepherds, in the field abiding,
Watching o'er your flocks by night,
God with us is now residing;
Yonder shines the infant light:

Sages, leave your contemplations,
Brighter visions beam afar;
Seek the great Desire of nations;
Ye have seen His natal star.

Saints, before the altar bending,
Watching long in hope and fear;

Suddenly the Lord, descending,
In His temple shall appear.

Sinners, wrung with true repentance,
Doomed for guilt to endless pains,
Justice now revokes the sentence,
Mercy calls you; break your chains.

Though an Infant now we view Him,
He shall fill His Father's throne,
Gather all the nations to Him;
Every knee shall then bow down:

This carol was the most famous composition by poet and hymn writer James Montgomery. Montgomery was born in Irvine, Ayrshire, Scotland on the 4 November 1771, where his Irish father John was a minister in the Moravian Church, a denomination founded in fifteenth-century Bohemia, which is now largely the Czech Republic.

Members of the Moravian Church to this day place a high value on mission, unity, piety and music. In 1722 there was a 'revival' in the Church when a small group of Moravians, who had been living illegally in Bohemia were allowed to settle in what is now modern-day Germany. The town grew quickly and was seen as the centre for the mission of the Church. Hundreds of small 'renewal groups' were formed throughout Europe, they kept in regular contact and encouraged each other to maintain the growth in the Church.

Within thirty years the Moravian Church had sent out hundreds of missionaries throughout the world, to the Caribbean, North and South America, Africa, the Arctic and the East. The missionaries cared deeply about those who were oppressed in the Caribbean two Moravian missionaries even sold themselves into slavery to minister to the slaves.

When he was five years old, Montgomery's parents moved to the Moravian settlement at Gracehill, near Ballymena, County Antrim, Ireland. At seven years old he was sent off for training at Fulneck Seminary in Yorkshire where he made a profession of faith. Then in 1783, when he was only twelve years old, his parents were sent off to the West Indies as missionaries. Sadly, not long after they had arrived, both his parents died; his father is buried in Barbados and his mother in Tobago.

At the seminary, secular fiction and poetry were not allowed, but Montgomery found ways of borrowing and reading a large amount of poetry, including Burns and Milton. He wrote poetry of his own and planned to pen an epic poem when he was older. His school record was poor and in 1787 he was sent to work as an apprentice in a bakery in Mirfield, near Wakefield. The work didn't suit him and he moved to Rotherham to look for an alternative way to earn a living.

He travelled to London, hoping to find a publisher for his poetry, but this ended in failure. He did his best to support himself by any means available, usually 'precariously and dubiously' until 1792, when he became an assistant to Joseph Gale, auctioneer, bookseller and printer of the *Sheffield Register*.

The *Register* was a magazine that reported on local and national events and was set up by Gale in response to a request from Tom Paine, the famous English radical. The *Register* called for a free voice for all political dissenters, and campaigned against the excesses of the ruling classes. A year before Montgomery joined the *Register*, in 1791, Gale had given support to local artisans and small business holders who were opposed to the Enclosure Act, which meant that 6,000 acres of land was to be seized without compensation to the owners. With other campaigners, Gale continued to call for parliamentary reform. By 1794, William Pitt and his government feared that there would be violence from Sheffield because the Reformers had ceased to petition parliament, feeling that it was a fruitless exercise. Arrests and convictions started, with many being convicted of sedition and sentences of transportation for between seven and fourteen years were handed down. Gale criticised the arrests in the *Register*.

Knowing that he would be next, Gale fled to France to avoid prosecution and Montgomery took charge of the *Register*, changing its name to the *Sheffield Iris*. Even so, he was imprisoned for two months for an alleged libel Gale had made. When he was released, the authorities turned their attention to several articles on the French Revolution, commemorating the fall of the Bastille, and reports he had made of a riot, precipitated by soldiers, who fired on the demonstrators, killing two. The article and report were considered to be libellous and Montgomery was jailed once again, this time for six months.

To help the time pass, he wrote a small book entitled *Prison Amusements*, which he published on his release. When he was released, the success of the book led to such popularity that he became a leading citizen of Sheffield. More interestingly however, he had captured the imagination and hearts of the people.

At his own request, Montgomery was readmitted to the Moravian congregation at Fulneck in 1814, where he developed his faith and social conscience, allowing them to inform his work and the activities of the *Sheffield Iris*. He continued to campaign for parliamentary reform, the abolition of slavery, and was always ready to assist the downtrodden, poor and needy.

His most famous work, 'Angels from the Realms of Glory', was first printed in the *Sheffield Iris* on Christmas Eve, 1816.

In 1822, Montgomery's hymns were published in three volumes called *Songs of Zion: Being Imitations of Psalms*. They were immediately celebrated as laying the foundations for modern hymn writing. His work was described as, 'one central creative thought, shaping for itself melodious utterance, and with every detail subordinate to its harmonious presentation.'

In 1825, a rival took over the *Sheffield Iris*, leaving Montgomery time to devote to the completion of hymns. He produced over 400 hymns and skilfully adapted many more; around one hundred are still in use. There is no evidence that Montgomery wrote 'Angels from the Realms of Glory' in prison, however it is clear that he did write many hymns around that time. There have been suggestions that he may well have written his hymn 'Lift up Ye Heads, Ye Gates of Brass' there, although this almost certainly meant to be humourous rather than historically accurate. The title and some of the verses relate to Psalm 24:7 in the Bible:

> Lift up your heads, O you gates;
> be lifted up, you ancient doors,
> that the King of glory may come in.

Montgomery also wrote secular poetry, lecturing at the Royal Institution. The lectures were subsequently published under the title *Lectures on Poetry and General Literature* in 1833. The poems denounced the practice of slavery and brought him notoriety far beyond his city of Sheffield. His epic poem, 'The Wanderer of Switzerland' tells, in six parts, the story of what Montgomery describes as:

> A Wanderer of Switzerland and his family, consisting of his wife, their daughter and her young children, emigrating from their country in consequence of its' subjugation to the French in 1798, arriving at the cottage of a shepherd, beyond the frontiers, where they are hospitably entertained.

The poem was heavily criticised by the *Edinburgh Review*, but favourably accepted by the poet Byron. With a degree of insight, when Montgomery was asked which of his poems would stand the test of time, he responded, 'None, Sir, nothing except perhaps a few of my hymns'.

In the later years of his life, he was awarded an annual pension of £200 by the government for his 'contribution to society', presumably as some atonement for his imprisonment. He was also heavily involved with the promotion of religious and philanthropic movements and he kept his enthusiasm for speaking publically against injustice and intolerance. He never married, and died quietly in his sleep at home in Sheffield, on 30 April 1854 at the age of 83, the day after he had written what was to be his last hymn. He was buried in Sheffield following a public funeral in the city, and a statue was erected, a stained-glass window was installed in the parish church, and a public hall was named in his memory.

Following the tragic start to his life, James Montgomery battled against all odds to become a successful radical, civic figure and prolific hymn writer. He should be widely regarded as a hero for those who continue to struggle against injustice.

10

Silent Night, Holy Night

(Popular)
Silent night, holy night
All is calm, all is bright
Round yon Virgin Mother and Child
Holy Infant so tender and mild
Sleep in heavenly peace
Sleep in heavenly peace

Silent night, holy night!
Shepherds quake at the sight
Glories stream from heaven afar
Heavenly hosts sing
Alleluia! Christ, the Saviour is born
Christ, the Saviour is born

Silent night, holy night
Son of God, love's pure light
Radiant beams from Thy holy face
With the dawn of redeeming grace
Jesus, Lord, at Thy birth
Jesus, Lord, at Thy birth '

(Complete – Translated from the German
Stille Nacht! Heilige Nacht)

Silent night! Holy night!
All's asleep, one sole light,
Just the faithful and holy pair,
Lovely boy-child with curly hair,
Sleep in heavenly peace!
Sleep in heavenly peace!

Silent night! Holy night!
God's Son laughs, o how bright.
Love from your holy lips shines clear,
As the dawn of salvation draws near,
Jesus, Lord, with your birth!
Jesus, Lord, with your birth!

Silent night! Holy night!
Brought the world peace tonight,
From the heavens' golden height
Shows the grace of His holy might
Jesus, as man on this earth!
Jesus, as man on this earth!

Silent night! holy night!
Where today all the might
Of His fatherly love us graced
And then Jesus, as brother embraced.
All the peoples on earth!
All the peoples on earth!

Silent night! Holy night!
Long we hoped that He might,
As our Lord, free us of wrath,

Since times of our fathers He hath
Promised to spare all mankind!
Promised to spare all mankind!

Silent night! Holy night!
Shepherds first see the sight.
Told by angelic Alleluia,
Sounding everywhere, both near and far:
'Christ the Saviour is here!'
'Christ the Saviour is here!'

Written by Joseph Mohr with a melody by Franz Xaver Gruber, 'Silent Night, Holy Night' was first performed at Midnight Mass on Christmas Eve 1818 in Nikolaus-Kirche (St Nicholas' Church) in Oberndorf, Austria. Since then, the carol has enjoyed worldwide popularity; it is said there are over 300 translations of it in existence, even a basic search of the Internet will turn up over 200 versions in at least 150 different languages.

It all started when Fr Joseph Mohr, Franz Xaver Gruber, the parish curate and the choir director sang the carol accompanied by a guitar. At the end of each of the six verses, the choir would repeat the last two lines in four-part harmony. It was rather unique that a guitar would be used in church at the time, but the simplicity of the tune was suitable for such accompaniment.

The German words for the original six verses were written two years earlier in 1816 by Mohr, when he was posted to a mission church in Mariapfarr, Austria. Eventually, he took them to Gruber, with the intention of performing the carol at midnight mass, asking that he might write a composition, suitable for the service. In his written account, Gruber gives no mention of any inspiration he might have had for creating the tune.

Joseph Mohr.

There are many myths surrounding the creation of this carol and its unusual original accompaniment. One suggests that mice had chewed through parts of the organ, so that it was unusable. This particular story appeared in 1965, although it was part of a common myth before that. There was even a drama-tised television documentary called *Silent Mouse* that appeared on television in 1988, telling the story of the creation of the carol from the mouse's point of view. Similarly, there is a story that suggests that the lyrics and the music were subsequently forgotten by Gruber and Mohr, only to be rediscovered later by an organ repairer. This myth is easily discounted, as there are various musical arrangements and changes to the lyrics, pro-duced by Mohr and Gruber.

It is much more likely that Mohr simply wanted to produce a new Christmas carol, simple and easily sung, to the accom-

An English translation of 'Silent Night'. (New York : American Book Company, 1905)

paniment of a guitar. Gruber's composition reflects the rural folk music that would have been common at the time. The original manuscript has been lost. However, the earliest, clearly in Mohr's handwriting, dates back to around 1820.

The man who translated 'Stille Nacht' into 'Silent Night' was John Freeman Young, whilst assigned to Trinity Church, New York City. Young was born in 1820, two years after the first public performance of the carol. Converting to the Anglican Church from his Methodist background, he attended Theological Seminary, eventually starting ministry in Jacksonville, Florida. At the time he was one of only two paid clergy in the state. He moved to various posts in the South – Texas, Mississippi and Louisiana – until in 1855 he arrived in New York City. This was a busy time in his life; he enjoyed church architecture, hymnology and translating famous hymns from various churches, including 'Silent Night', in 1859, which appeared in a sixteen-page pamphlet entitled Carols for Christmastide. In 1867, the Revd Young was consecrated as Bishop of Florida.

There is a fourth verse wrongly attributed to Bishop Young:

> Silent night, Holy night,
> Wondrous star, lend thy light
> With the angels let us sing

Alleluia to our King
Christ the Saviour is here,
Jesus the Saviour is here!

This verse remains anonymous, although those who love this hymn are still hoping that a manuscript will appear to confirm the identity of the person who added the verse. To this day, 'Silent Night, Holy Night' remains a firm favourite and regularly appears at the top of favourite Christmas Carol polls. Since being written, set to music and performed, it has grown in popularity to become a truly universal carol.

In the chapter on 'O Come All Ye Faithful', we looked at the carols sung in the trenches during the 1914 First World War ceasefire and 'Silent Night, Holy Night' was reportedly sung simultaneously in English, French and German according to Stanley Weintraub on the 1914 truce *Silent Night: The Remarkable Christmas Truce of 1914* (2001). It has been performed and recorded by many, among them; Johnny Cash, Elvis Presley, Stevie Nicks, Bing Crosby, Tori Amos, Christina Aguilera, Westlife and most recently Susan Boyle and Annie Lennox. It has been rearranged, parodied and performed by choirs, orchestras and buskers!

11

Once in Royal David's City

Once in royal David's city,
Stood a lowly cattle shed,
Where a mother laid her Baby,
In a manger for His bed:
Mary was that mother mild,
Jesus Christ, her little Child.

He came down to earth from heaven,
Who is God and Lord of all,
And His shelter was a stable,
And His cradle was a stall:
With the poor, and mean, and lowly,
Lived on earth our Saviour holy.

For He is our childhood's pattern;
Day by day, like us, He grew;
He was little, weak, and helpless,
Tears and smiles, like us He knew;
And He cares when we are sad,
And he shares when we are glad.

And our eyes at last shall see Him,
Through His own redeeming love;
For that Child so dear and gentle,
Is our Lord in heaven above:
And He leads His children on,
To the place where He is gone.

For millions of listeners all over the world, Christmas begins with the clear treble voice of a Cambridge choirboy. Every year since 1919 this has been the opening hymn in the service of Nine Lessons and Carols, broadcast from King's College chapel on Christmas Eve. The hymn itself is much older than the service, written for a collection of hymns more than half a century earlier.

The hymn writer, Cecil Frances Alexander, was born in early April 1818, the second daughter of Major John Humphries of County Tyrone, Ireland. As a child, she started to write religious verse and was strongly influenced by John Keble and other members of the Oxford Movement; many years later Keble himself would edit one of her anthologies. Many hymn writers of the day felt the same affinity to the Oxford Movement, who were high church Anglicans who argued for the reinstatement of traditional liturgy, symbolism and theology. She would have been in good company with her peers, John Mason Neale, who wrote 'Good King Wenceslas', and Christina Rossetti, who wrote 'In the Bleak Midwinter', all of whom were influenced by the traditional church and the Oxford Movement.

In 1850, when she married the Revd William Alexander, the thirty-two-year-old Cecil Frances (Fanny) Humphries was already a published hymn writer, with her *Hymns for Little Children* published two years earlier. This collection included the favourite 'All Things Bright and Beautiful', 'There is a Green Hill Far Away', and the carol 'Once in Royal David's City', written to help children imagine the circumstances in

Hymns for Little Children by C.F. Alexander (1848). This cover from the 1903 edition with artwork by Joan and Dorothea Drew.

which Jesus Christ was born, and to illustrate the words of the Apostles Creed, an early statement of Christian belief, probably written down by St Ambrose in around AD 390.

When they married, Revd William Alexander, who had been educated in Brasenose College, Oxford, held several parishes before becoming the Bishop of Derry and Raphoe in 1867. He was well regarded for his preaching and theological insights; in 1871 he was saddened to be the last bishop to sit in the House of Lords before Disestablishment under the Irish Churches Act. In 1896 he was elevated to the most senior Church position when he became the Archbishop of Ireland.

On the day of the Disestablishment of the Church of Ireland, a hymn written by Cecil Alexander was sung in her husband's cathedral, which included the controversial verse:

Look down, Lord of heaven on our desolation,
Fallen, fallen, fallen is now our Country's crown,
Dimly down the New year as a Churchless nation,
Mammon and Amalek tread our borders down.

Alexander continues to this day to attract controversy for her lyrics. Her conservative values on the place of the poor in society, which was by no means extraordinary at the time, has resulted in the following verse from 'All Things Bright and Beautiful' being removed from most hymn books:

> The rich man in his castle,
> The poor man at his gate,
> God made them, high and lowly,
> And order'd their estate.

Even without this verse, the hymn remains a favourite for many occasions including weddings and funerals.

Alexander held with the common belief amongst middle-class Victorians that 'the poor were improvident, they wasted any money they had on drink and gambling' and that 'God had put people in their place in life and this must not be interfered with because the life after death was more important'. Nevertheless, she was extremely generous and donated all payments for her poetry to Derry and Raphoe Diocesan Institution for the Deaf and Dumb, which was founded in 1846 in Strabane.

Cecil Frances Alexander wrote more than 400 hymns during her life, including what could be arguably said to be the most famous carol of all time, 'Once in Royal David's City'. Her book for children was in its 69th edition by the late nineteenth century, and throughout the world people were familiar with her work.

Later in her life, she translated the sixth-century prayer to be said before a journey, traditionally attributed to St Patrick. The popular 'St Patrick's Breastplate' begins with the old Irish:

> *Atomriug indiu*
> *niurt tríun*

Statue of St Patrick.

togairm Tríndóite
cretim treodatad
fóisitin oendatad
i nDúilemon dáil.

Alexander translated and created a metrical version of the prayer to be used as a hymn. The first verse begins:

Christ be with me, Christ within me, Christ behind me, Christ before me, Christ beside me, Christ to win me, Christ to comfort and restore me. Christ beneath me, Christ above me, Christ in quiet, Christ in danger, Christ in hearts of all that love me, Christ in mouth of friend and stranger.

They were married for forty-five years, half of which was lived in Derry. She died in Dublin in 1895, and is buried in the City Cemetery in Londonderry.

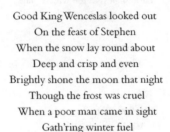

Good King Wenceslas

12

Good King Wenceslas looked out
On the feast of Stephen
When the snow lay round about
Deep and crisp and even
Brightly shone the moon that night
Though the frost was cruel
When a poor man came in sight
Gath'ring winter fuel

'Hither, page, and stand by me
If thou know'st it, telling
Yonder peasant, who is he?
Where and what his dwelling?'
'Sire, he lives a good league hence
Underneath the mountain
Right against the forest fence
By Saint Agnes' fountain.'

'Bring me flesh and bring me wine
Bring me pine logs hither
Thou and I will see him dine

When we bear him thither.'
Page and monarch forth they went
Forth they went together
Through the rude wind's wild lament
And the bitter weather

'Sire, the night is darker now
And the wind blows stronger
Fails my heart, I know not how,
I can go no longer.'
'Mark my footsteps, my good page
Tread thou in them boldly
Thou shalt find the winter's rage
Freeze thy blood less coldly.'

In his master's steps he trod
Where the snow lay dinted
Heat was in the very sod
Which the Saint had printed
Therefore, Christian men, be sure
Wealth or rank possessing
Ye who now will bless the poor
Shall yourselves find blessing.

Wenceslas Square is situated in Prague, the capital of the Czech Republic. Much has happened there; historically it was used as a horse market in the fourteenth century when the Bohemian King Charles IV founded the New Town of Prague. It was named Wenceslas Square in 1848. In 1918, a proclamation of independence was read there. Mass demonstrations were held in the square by the Nazis and in 1945, from the 5-8 May, many of the buildings around the square were damaged as the Czech Resistance attempted to gain control just before the Red Army arrived at the end of the Second World War in

Europe. In 1969 a student, Jan Palach, set fire to himself to protest about the invasion of Czechoslovakia by the Soviet Union in 1968. In 1989, during the 'Velvet Revolution' (known as the 'Gentle Revolution' in the Czech Republic), many demonstrations were held there, leading to democratic elections in 1990. Wenceslas Square and Wenceslas its namesake are important to the people of the Czech Republic, and indeed to the world, as it is now a UNESCO World Heritage Site, but who was he? Was Wenceslas a king, a duke or a saint? Why does his statue dominate the square, and why has he a place that is foremost in the national life of the Czech Republic named after him?

In the late ninth century, Saints Cyril and Methodius undertook missionary journeys throughout central and eastern Europe amongst the Slavic peoples. The Czech Duke Borivoy and his wife Ludmilla were converted on one of these missions although many people were opposed to the introduction of

A statue of Wenceslas in Prague.

Christianity, as it threatened the ancient religion practiced in that region. The son of Borivoy and Ludmilla, Prince Vratislav, married Drahomira, the daughter of a pagan tribal chief, who held tenaciously to the ancient beliefs. Their first son, Wenceslas, was born near Prague in 907.

When Wenceslas was thirteen, his father was killed in a battle. Drahomira, his mother, took advantage of the power vacuum and religious animosity to gain support from the powerful pagan nobility whilst Wenceslas was still too young to rule. During that time, his grandmother, Ludmilla, arranged to bring him up; carefully ensuring that he kept his Christian faith, being taught by a priest who was a disciple of St Methodius. This enraged Drahomira, and she conceived a plan to murder Ludmilla, who was strangled shortly after.

Feeling herself now exempt from all Christian duty, the mother reclaimed her son. Secretly, however, Wenceslas continued to practice his Christian faith. Eventually an uprising deposed and banished Drahomira, leaving Wenceslas to take power at the age of eighteen. Wenceslas however, recalled his mother to the castle and forgave her.

There followed stories of great bravery and generosity, as Wenceslas spent much of his wealth supporting the needy in and around the city. There were also stories of miracles, where people were healed from various disabilities. The carol recounts one such incident, where Wenceslas left his bed one night and ordered his trusted knight Podiven to follow him as he delivered alms to the poor. This was a particularly foolhardy endeavour in the snow and ice. At one stage Podiven was about to give up because his feet were numb with the cold, then Wenceslas told him to walk in his footprints, which became miraculously warm. The alms were delivered and the pair returned to the castle. Wenceslas was legendary amongst his people, and considered to be a man of high integrity and morals.

However, it was his ambitious program to build churches that enraged the nobility. The troubles were soon to erupt again in earnest.

Although Wenceslas was reconciled to his mother, his younger brother Boleslas began to challenge him. The birth of Wenceslas' first son stirred up jealousy, as succession would now pass to him rather than Boleslas. A plan was devised to kill Wenceslas after a church service, that Boleslas was certain he would attend. After the service, Boleslas followed him out and he was hacked to pieces by his servants on the steps of the cathedral.

Wenceslas was considered a saint and martyr immediately after his death, and within a few years hagiographies were written of his life. These 'biographies' of the saints had a huge influence of the people of the High Middle Ages. Wenceslas was used to support the belief that legitimate authority does not automatically arise from the divine right of kings, a ruler needs to be able to demonstrate that they are *rex justus*, a righteous king, stemming not only from great piety but princely vigour.

Referring to these hagiographies, one writer, Cosmas of Prague writing in the year 1119 agrees:

> But his deeds I think you know better than I could tell you; for, as is read in his Passion, no one doubts that, rising every night from his noble bed, with bare feet and only one chamberlain, he went around to God's churches and gave alms generously to widows, orphans, those in prison and afflicted by every difficulty, so much so that he was considered, not a prince, but the father of all the wretched.

On the question of whether Wenceslas was a duke, king or saint, the answer is that he was all three. During his lifetime he was a duke, posthumously the Holy Roman Emperor Otto I made him 'king'. He was also canonized as a saint due to his martyr's death, as well as for several purported miracles that occurred after his death. Wenceslas is the patron saint of the Czech people and the Czech Republic and his feast day is 28 September; in 2000 it was declared a permanent public holiday in the Czech Republic, celebrated as Czech Statehood Day.

The story doesn't end there though, the carol 'Good King Wenceslas', written by the eminent English clergyman and author John Mason Neale, has a story all of its own. Neale was born in London in 1818. His father died when he was five years old. When he was fourteen he began to translate the poetical writings of Coelius Sedulius, who wrote around AD 450, and was thought to be one of the founders of Christian hymn writing. While a student Neale developed an extraordinary interest in church archaeology, especially architecture, and

John Mason Neale.

with a few others founded the Cambridge Camden Society in 1839, renamed the Ecclesiological Society, which exercised an immense influence on the architecture and ritual of the English Church, which lasted till 1845.

Neale was a great supporter of 'Victorian Gothic' and worked ceaselessly with those who wanted more ritual and religious decoration in churches. This movement was a natural partner to Tractarianism (the Oxford Movement) as both looked back to the Middle Ages as a time when the church met the needs of its parishioners both spiritually and aesthetically.

Neale graduated from Trinity College, Cambridge in 1840. He was ordained deacon in 1841 and priest in 1842. 1842 was also the year he met and married Sarah Webster. They moved to Crawley, Surrey, where he became incumbent. Ill health meant that Neale needed to resign within a few months and they went to live in Madeira.

Fortunately for Neale and hymn writing, there was a fine library at the cathedral there, from which he found sources for one of his books *History of the Eastern Church*, and also for his Commentary on the Psalms.

He returned to England in 1845, and from 1846 until his death he was Warden of Sackville College, East Grinstead, Sussex. In fact, the college was an almshouse, a charitable institution for the aged. Neale's salary was a mere £27 a year. There he wrote furiously; history, theology, travel books, hymns, poems and books for children.

Neale continued to be a traditionalist and a staunch supporter of the Oxford Movement, this attracted criticism from many quarters, as did his outspoken views on the judgment of God that would fall on those clergy who took and destroyed consecrated property from the churches, installing 'pews' and other innovations. His criticism of wealthy clergy living in luxurious surroundings and his insistence on traditional

The title page of
Piae Cantiones.

church furnishings meant that for the last few years of his life
he was censured by his bishop, and prevented from ministering
in Church. Working closely with those who had little worldly
goods in the 'college', supporting antiquarians who were
intent on preserving the churches and continuing to act as a
minister, it's quite easy to see how Neale was drawn to the
story of Good King Wenceslas.

Neale wrote the lyrics for 'Good King Wenceslas' to the tune
of a thirteenth-century spring song 'Tempus Adest Floridum'
('It is time for Flowering'), which was first published in the
sixteenth century Finnish collection *Piae Cantiones*. The first
appearance of the carol in print was in the book *Carols for
Christmastide*, which Neale published with Thomas Helmore in

1853. It is highly likely, however, that he had written the carol sometime earlier, possibly when he completed his book *Deeds of Faith* in 1849, which Neale wrote to 'to lead children to take an interest in Ecclesiastical History' through sixteen stories of saints and martyrs, including 'The Legend of St. Wenceslaus'.

Neale says of Wenceslas, on his mission to the poor on the Feast of Stephen:

> And so great was the virtue of this Saint of the Most High, such was the fire of love that was kindled in him, that, as he trod in those steps, [his knight Podiven] gained life and heat. He felt not the wind; he heeded not the frost; the footprints glowed as with a holy fire, and zealously he followed the King on his errand of mercy.

Perhaps Neale was drawn to the legend of Wenceslas because they shared the tragic loss of their fathers at an early age? Perhaps he saw the 'King' as someone who would uphold the faith in the face of trouble and conflict, as Neale felt he was doing? Whatever the reason, Neale has succeeded in his purpose, to this day people still sing of Good King Wenceslas, the unlikely hero of the poor and needy.

13

In the Bleak Midwinter

In the bleak midwinter
Frosty wind made moan,
Earth stood hard as iron,
Water like a stone;
Snow had fallen, snow on snow,
Snow on snow,
In the bleak midwinter,
Long ago.

Our God, heaven cannot hold him,
Nor earth sustain;
Heaven and earth shall flee away
When he comes to reign;
In the bleak midwinter
A stable place sufficed
The Lord God incarnate,
Jesus Christ.

Enough for him, whom Cherubim
Worship night and day
A breast full of milk

And a manger full of hay.
Enough for him, whom angels
Fall down before,
The ox and ass and camel
Which adore.

Angels and archangels
May have gathered there,
Cherubim and seraphim
Thronged the air;
But his mother only,
In her maiden bliss,
Worshipped the Beloved
With a kiss.

What can I give him,
Poor as I am?
If I were a shepherd
I would bring a lamb,
If I were a wise man
I would do my part,
Yet what I can I give Him
Give my heart.

Christina Georgina Rossetti was one of the most important women poets writing in the nineteenth century. Born
in London on 5 December 1830 to Gabriele and Frances
Polidori Rossetti, she was the fourth of five children. Her
father was an Italian patriot, exiled from Naples for his political activity, and a Dante scholar who became professor of
Italian at King's College, London, in 1831. At home, Christina
would have been fluent in both English and Italian. As part
of the large Italian expatriate community in London, they
welcomed other exiles, from Mazzini, the famous politi-

Christina Rossetti sketched
by her brother Dante.

cian in exile, to chimney sweeps; and although they were
certainly not wealthy, Professor Rossetti was able to support
the family comfortably.

Christina Rossetti's family were well-known poets, artists
and critics, and as a child she would have been surrounded
by people who were passionate about art, politics and religion. Although she spent most of her childhood in a dark
and depressing early Victorian London, she was exposed to
nature and the countryside on frequent visits to her grandfa-
ther. These themes recur throughout her poetry. Rossetti was
healthy as a child, but was often ill during adolescence. She was
diagnosed with 'a kind of religious mania' which might well
have been psychosomatic.

Sketches made of her by her brother Dante, who himself
became a famous artist, suggest that she was quite beautiful.
At eighteen years old she became engaged to James Collinson,
a young painter and member of the Pre-Raphaelite breth-
ren, but the engagement ended after he reverted to Roman
Catholicism in 1850. She, and the other Rossetti women,
were initially devout evangelical Anglicans, who were eventu-

ally drawn to the traditional call of the Tractarians. They did, however, keep their evangelical seriousness. Maria, one of her sisters, became a nun, and Christina's own religious poetry shows a deep commitment to her faith.

Rossetti continued her association with the Pre-Raphaelite movement. She herself was considered to have achieved the first success of the Pre-Raphaelite writers with the publication of *Goblin Market and Other Poems* in 1862. Rossetti often found herself caught between the worldly and the heavenly and this schism was central to her life and her poetry.

Her brother was able to convince Alexander Macmillan to publish three of Christina's poems in *Macmillian's Magazine*. One of the poems 'Uphill' was the first to receive attention and remains one of her finest works. This poem is an allegory about salvation, with the end being represented as an Inn.

Another of Rossetti's poems, 'The Iniquity of the Fathers Upon the Children' is a dramatic poem that deals with the issue of illegitimate children, by imagining that she herself is one. She had spent much time in charitable work at a home

The title page of the first edition of *Goblin Market*.

in Highgate, which was devoted to prostitutes and unmarried mothers. Much of her work at this time dealt with the chasm between the rich and poor, the injustice she witnessed on a daily basis and her desire for a fairer society.

Many writers have questioned what might have been if Rossetti hadn't been born into the early nineteenth century, where women poets and authors were silenced. In the male-centred culture in which she found herself, Rossetti challenged the status quo, creating her own world-view that provided fertile soil for her poetry and other women of the time. Her achievement cannot be underestimated; it is little known that at one stage she was seriously considered for Poet Laureate. Later in her career, Rossetti abandoned political subjects and concentrated more on the spiritual side of her art.

When her father's failing health and eyesight forced him to retire in 1853, Christina and her mother supported the family by starting a day school, but had to give it up after a year or so.

In the early 1860s she fell in love with Charles Cayley, who was famous for translating the work of Dante, an Italian poet of the Middle Ages, into English from the original. But according to her brother William, she refused to marry him because 'she enquired into his creed and found he was not a Christian.' After this she lived the life of a Victorian spinster, staying at home with her circle of her brother's friends which included author of *Alice in Wonderland*, Lewis Carroll; the American artist James Abbott MacNeil Whistler; and the English poet, playwright and novelist Algernon Charles Swinburne.

She continued to write and in the 1870s she worked for the Society for Promoting Christian Knowledge. Her brother Dante suffered a breakdown in 1872, which seriously affected her.

The poem 'In the Bleak Midwinter' was almost certainly written by Christina Rossetti around this time. It was published posthumously in 1906 not as a poem, but set to music by the English composer Gustav Holst as possibly one of the most atmospheric and moving Christmas carols of all time. Indeed in 2008, the setting by another English composer Harold Darke, which differs from Holst's arrangement by including a solo as the first verse, was voted the best carol according to the BBC *Music Magazine*, which questioned fifty-one directors of music in the UK and US. The deputy editor, Jeremy Pound, stated that the words were 'nigh on perfect as a carol text'.

The carol not only sets the Christmas scene in a beautifully descriptive way, it is also a complete guide to the Christian faith at Christmastime. In the first verse, Rossetti paints the picture of the circumstances of the birth of Jesus Christ in Bethlehem.

In verse two, Rossetti contrasts the incarnation with the second coming, stating that the birth was part of a cosmic plan, which would eventually bring about heaven on earth. She also highlights the poverty into which the child was born.

The third verse is a contrast, the cold harshness of the weather outside and the warmth of Mary in the stable. The presence of the animals also underlines the circumstances of the birth.

In the fourth verse, Rossetti gives us a touching picture of Mary kissing Jesus with great affection and a scene of invisible angels celebrating the birth. This reminds us that in the midst of such an important event there is something natural and genuine. This verse might have been a little mysterious for Darke, because it doesn't appear in his setting.

The final verse is, of course, an echo back to Rossetti's earlier work. She presents a challenge to those who would profess a faith, encouraging them to turn it to charitable works.

So, why do people suggest this is the best Christmas carol? Could it be the atmospheric scene setting? Could it be the simple but effective theology that explains the significance of the birth of Jesus Christ? Could it be the fact that it makes us think of those who live their lives in poverty, with love but little else to sustain them?

Some have suggested that the carol is 'depressing' and a 'Victorian dirge', however to many others, 'In the Bleak Midwinter' with the music of Holst and the words of Rossetti represents nothing less than the perfect Christmas carol.

This seems a fitting way to end our journey into the world of Christmas carols and songs. In this new millennium, I hope that we can continue to celebrate and enjoy Christmas each year, and feel good will for those around us.

Each Christmas, as the cold bites and bands of people wander the streets to sing carols and songs, we have the chance once again to believe in a better future, whilst enjoying the best of what the past has to offer in our villages, towns and cities. These tunes and lyrics are more than mere songs, they are the glue that can join communities together, creating a sense of shared concern, even if it only continues until the last cracker is pulled and the last mince pie is eaten.

May God bless you with an outrageously fun-filled Christmas, may you sing all your carols and songs in tune, and may Santa bring you more than you deserve!